CREATIVITY

ART, THE ARTIST & THE CHURCH

CREATIVITY

ART, THE ARTIST & THE CHURCH

CALEB PALMER

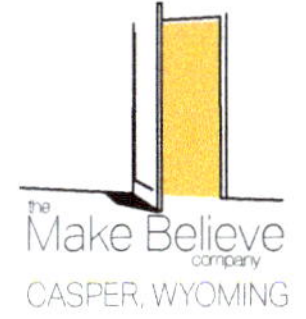

the Make Believe company
CASPER, WYOMING

ISBN 978-0-692-94671-8

Book set in Calluna.
Headings set in Avenir.
Edited by Anna Swartzentruber & Kathy Nickerson

Dedicated to:

My parents who taught me to dream,
My wife who dreams with me,
And my children who are my dream.

Thank you.

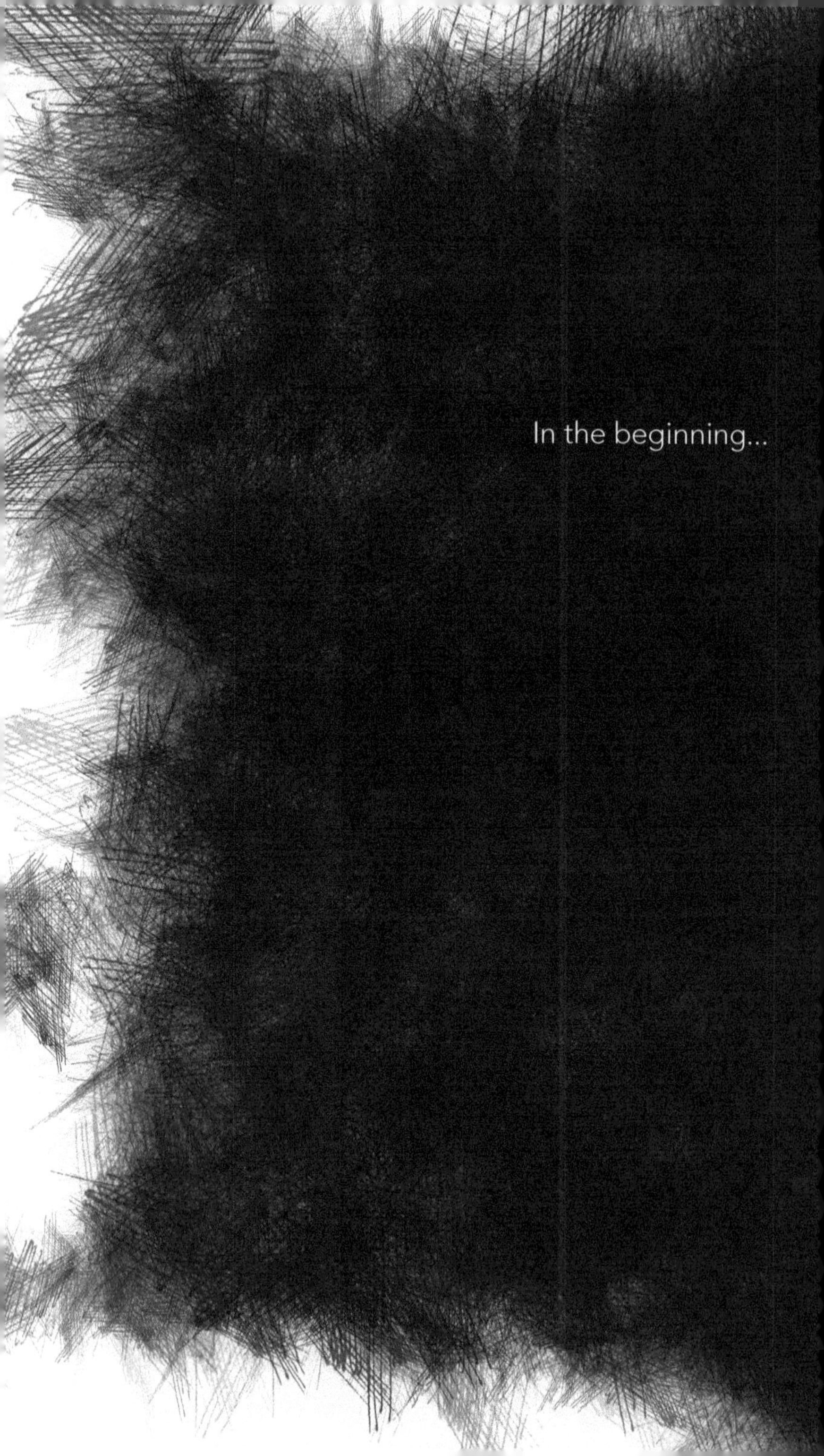

In the beginning...

Beginning — before anything else.

Not the beginning of a fine book,
or the beginning of a long road trip,
but the very beginning.

Before there was light,
before there was darkness,
before there was air,
before there was this corrupting force of sin
that so deeply entangles us.

Before our minds were given the capacity to
dream and imagine and conceive.

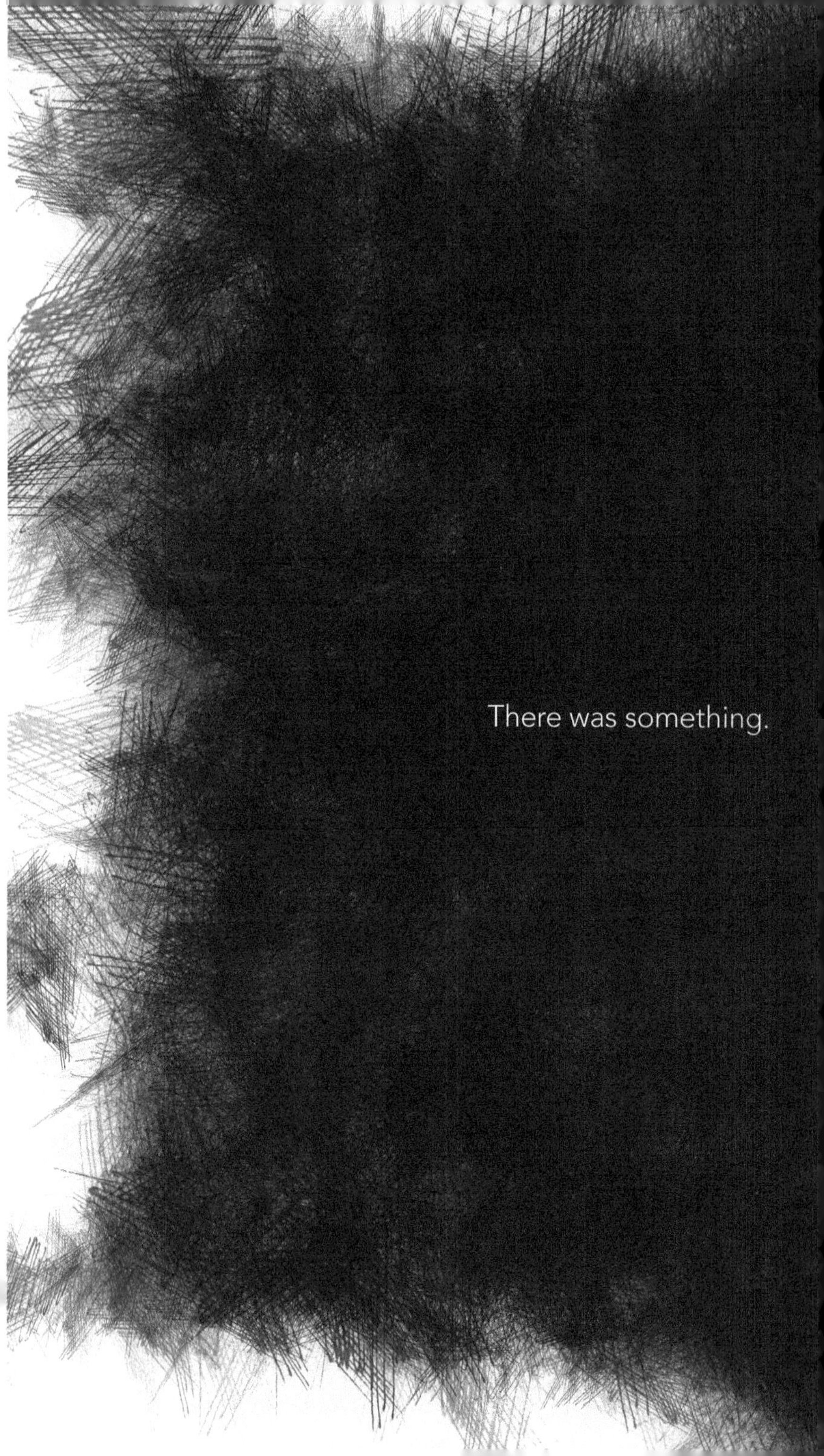
There was something.

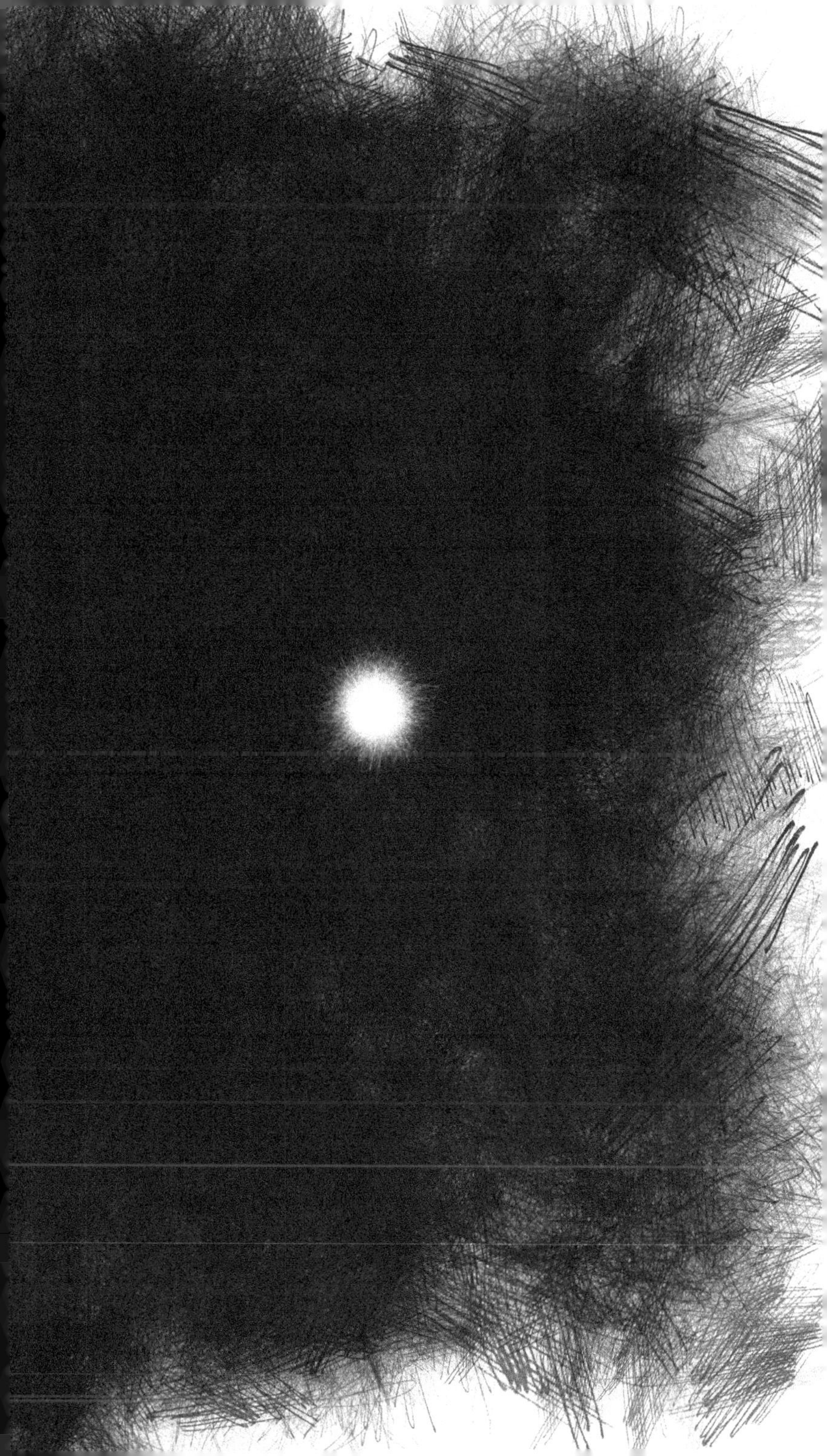

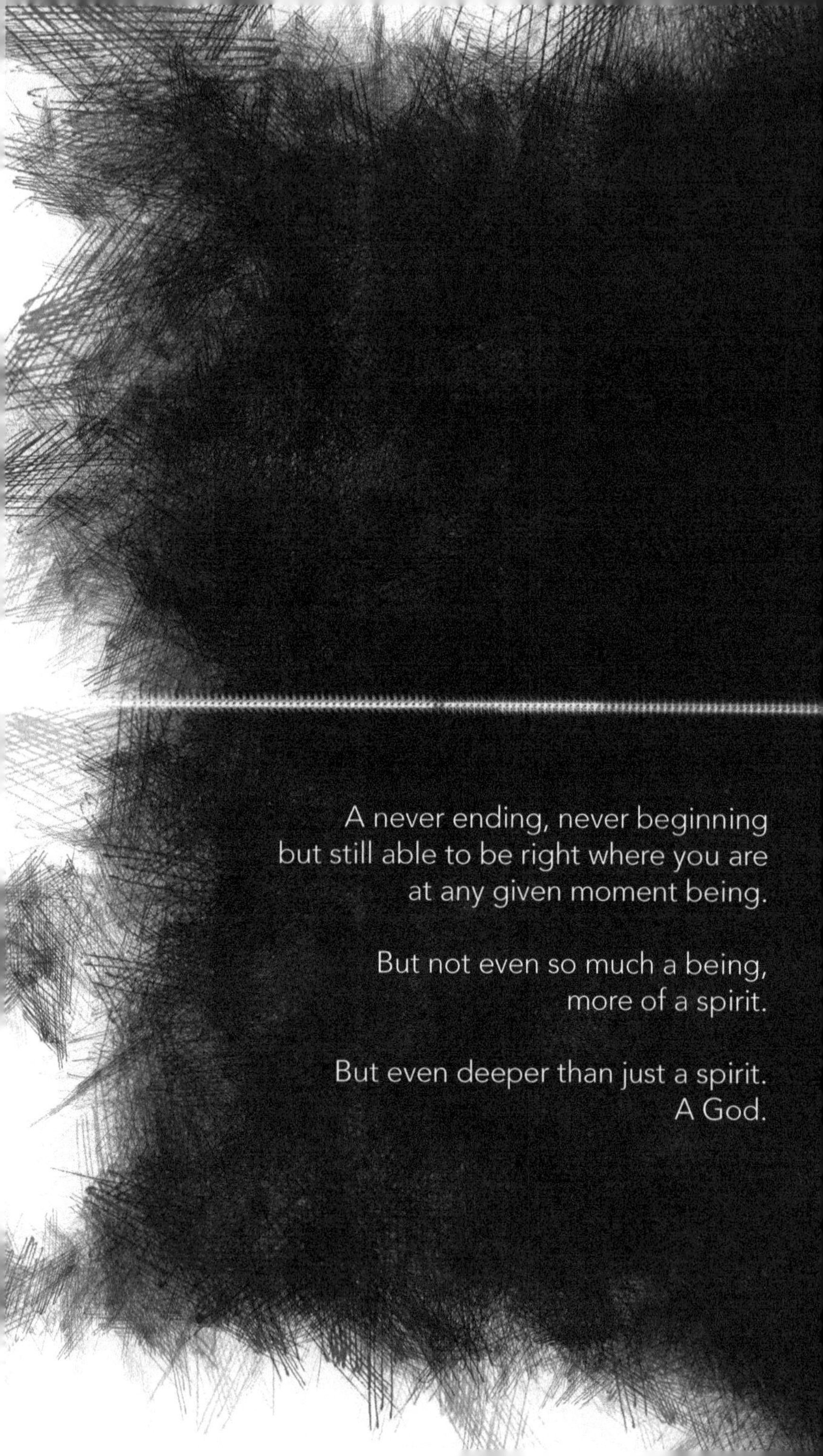

A never ending, never beginning
but still able to be right where you are
at any given moment being.

But not even so much a being,
more of a spirit.

But even deeper than just a spirit.
A God.

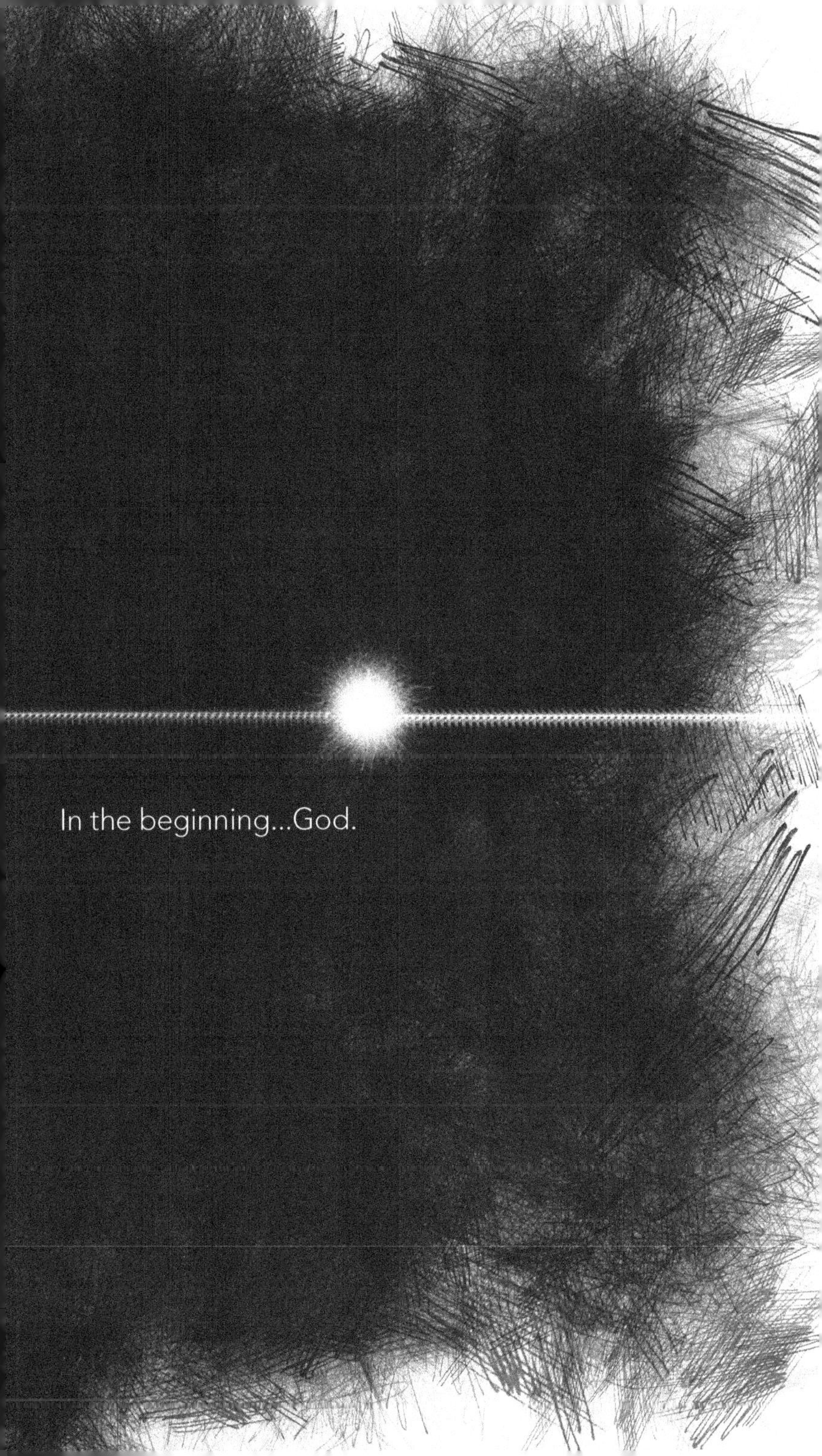
In the beginning...God.

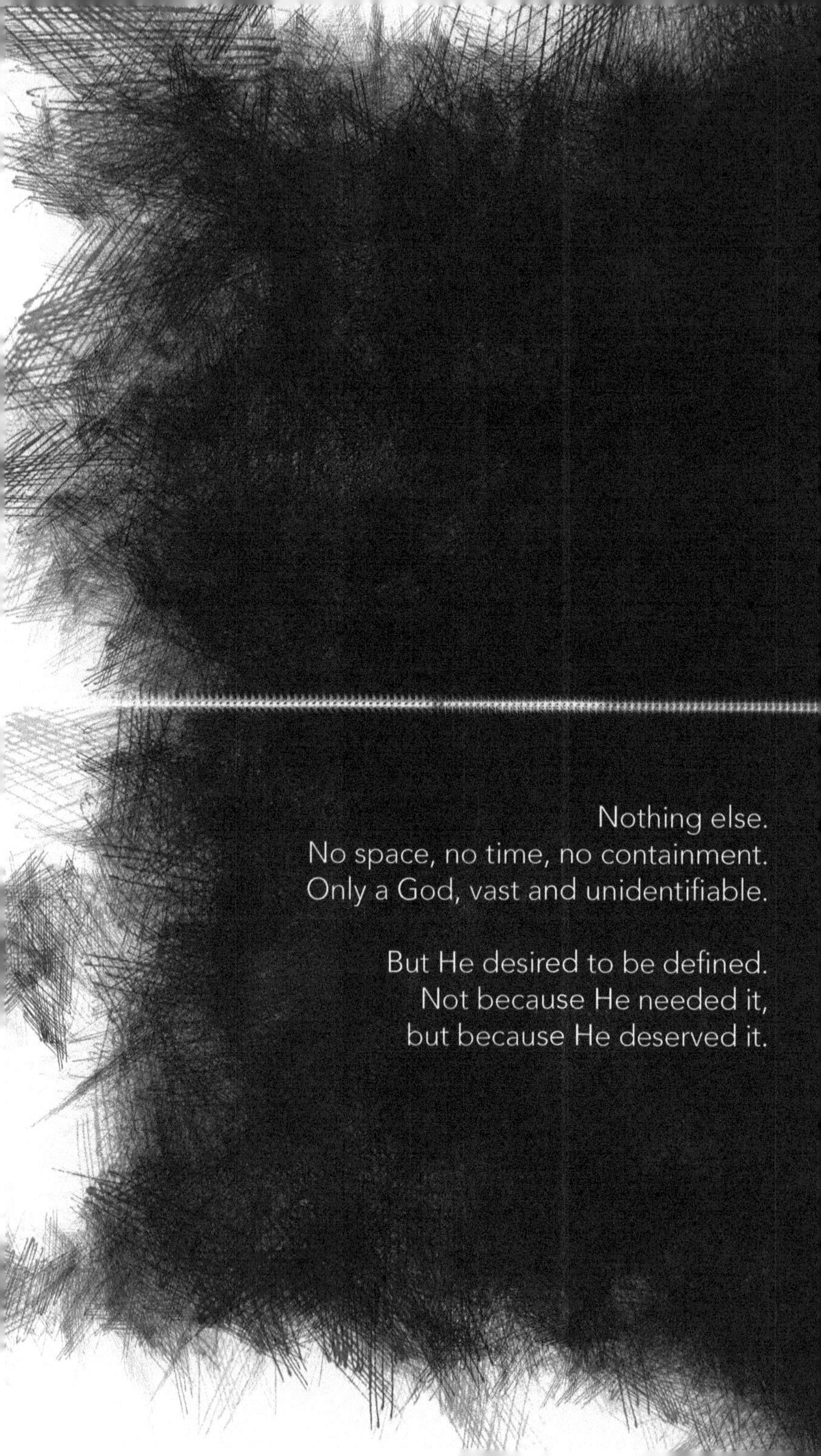
Nothing else.
No space, no time, no containment.
Only a God, vast and unidentifiable.

But He desired to be defined.
Not because He needed it,
but because He deserved it.

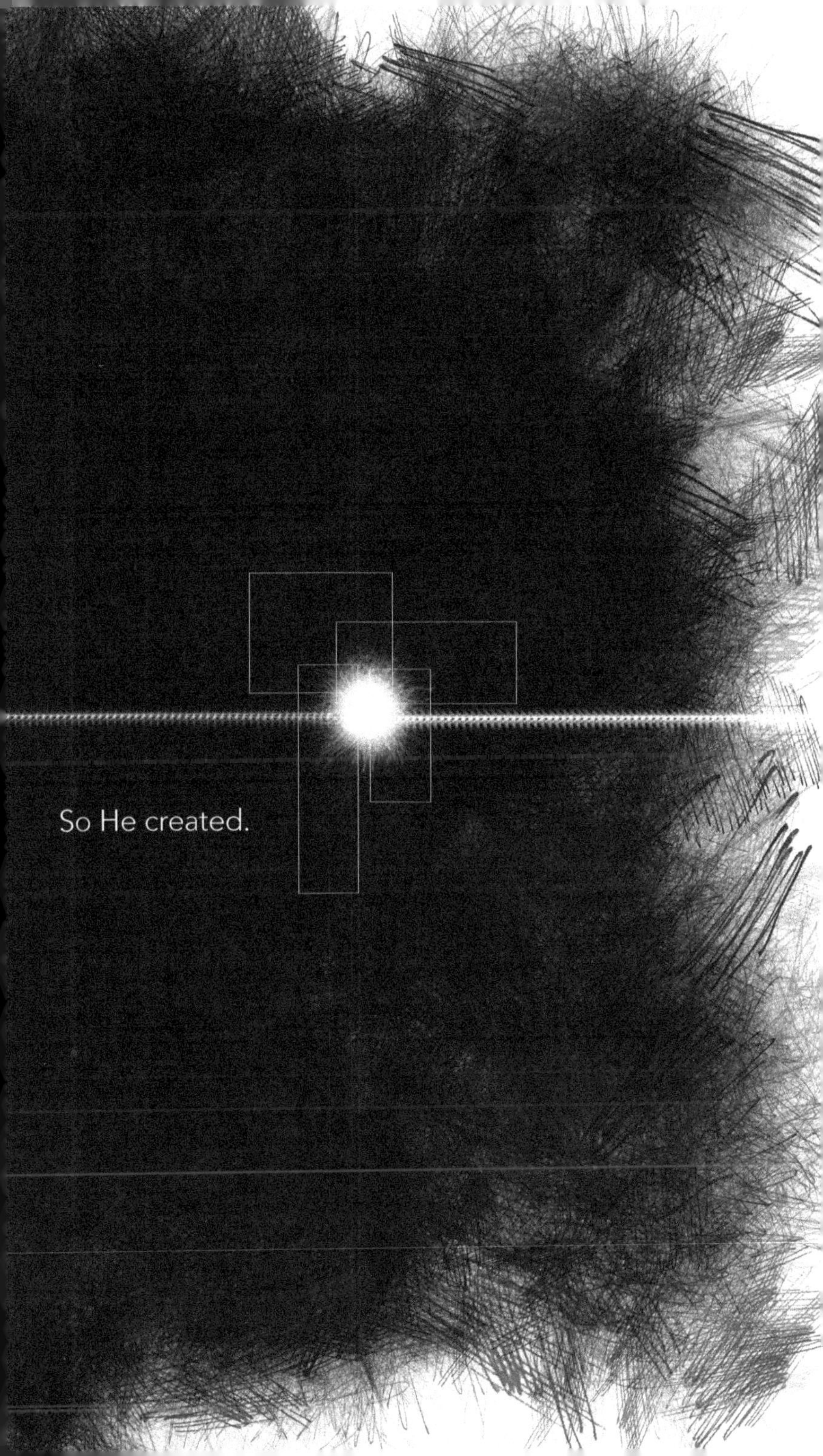

So He created.

He created the heavens and the earth.
A tangible, knowable, growing creation
whose sole purpose was to give Him glory.

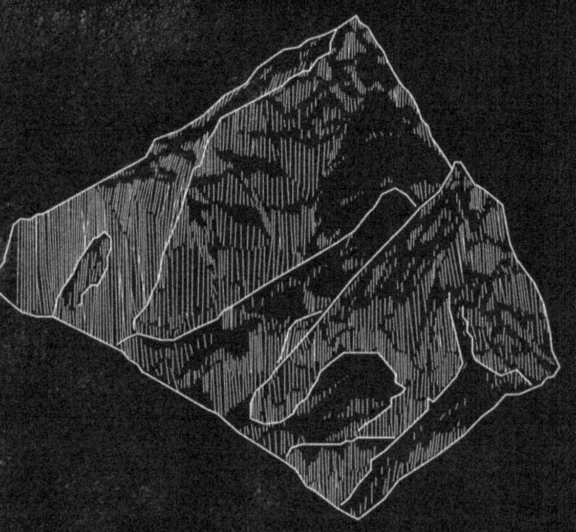

He created something with purpose.
He created something with reason.
He brought into being
out of nothing but Himself
every image,
every dream,
every picture
that we have ever seen or imagined.

And He did it in wisdom.

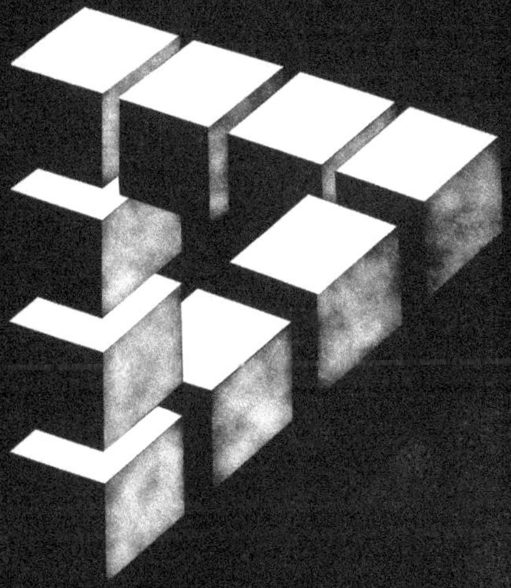

He took every possible combination
of every single dream that His uncontainable
mind could conceive
and created what was good.

That which was going to bring
Him the most glory.

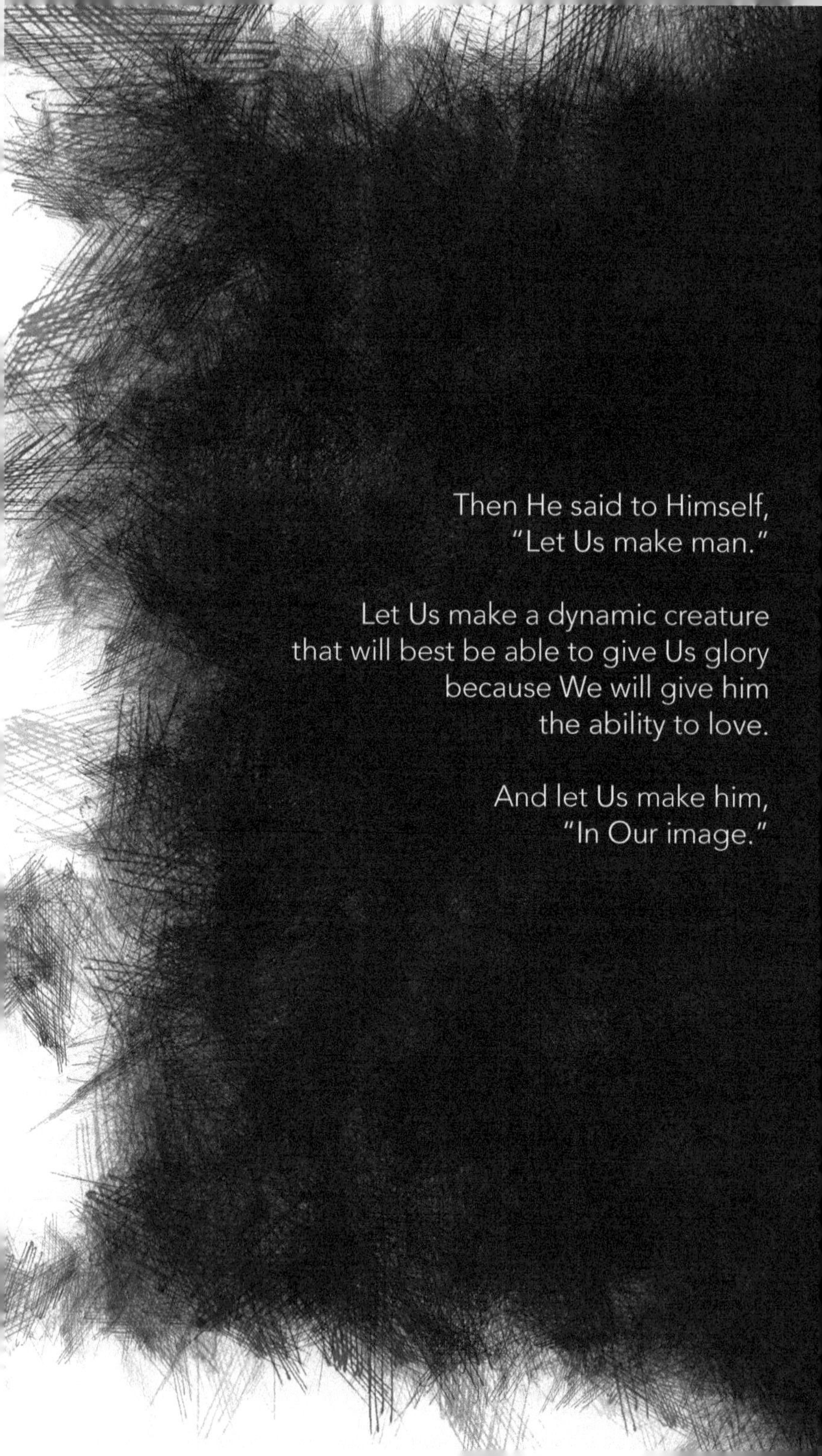

Then He said to Himself,
"Let Us make man."

Let Us make a dynamic creature
that will best be able to give Us glory
because We will give him
the ability to love.

And let Us make him,
"In Our image."

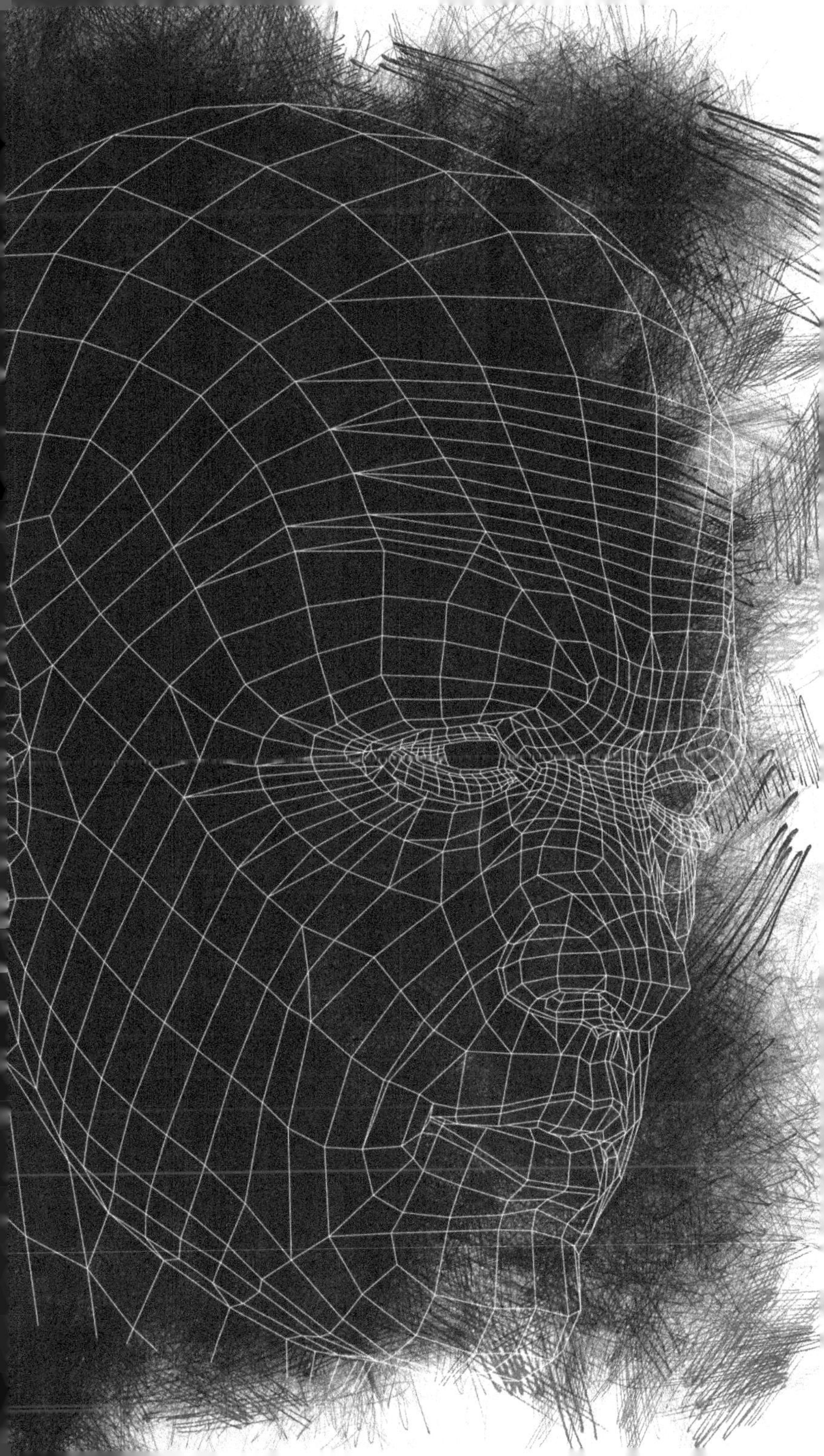

Let Us give him the ability to dream.
Let Us give him the ability to create.
Let Us instill on the inside of him
the same creative force that brought
this creation into being,
and although it will be only a reflection of Us,
it will be the great divider between
him and all My other creation.

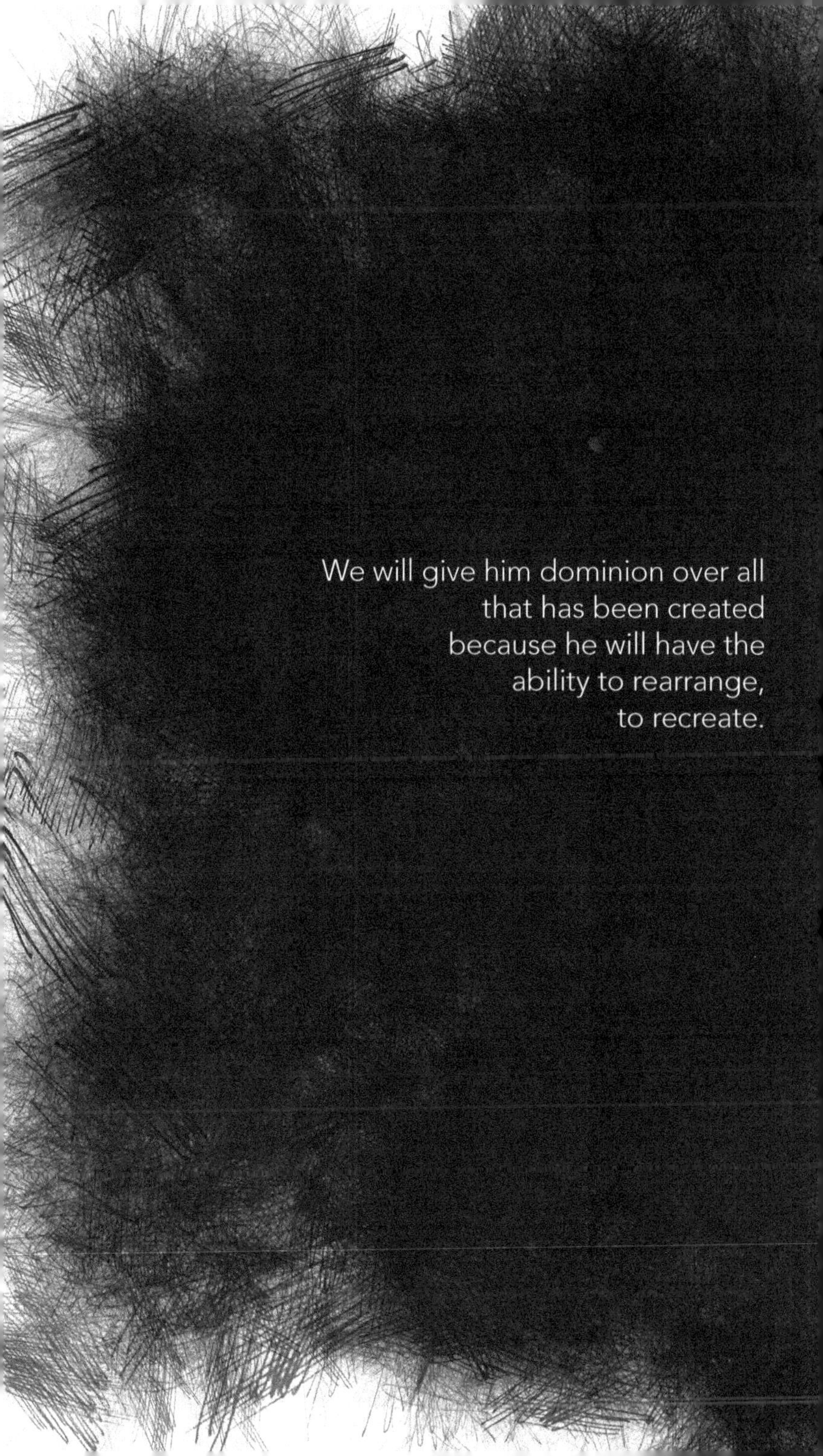

We will give him dominion over all
that has been created
because he will have the
ability to rearrange,
to recreate.

CREATING GODS/ CREATOR GOD

Gods are an interesting construct. For millennium, man has worked to define the hidden aspects of the world around us. There are things that we encounter that challenge our understanding. Each culture and people group throughout human history has had to deal with it. People groups with a close connection to the earth created gods that control the fundamental forces of nature. The Mayans, for example, had Ix Chel, the goddess of rainbows, which rather than being the sunny domain of unicorns and happiness, was, in fact, the flatulence of demons that brought bad luck and disease. The ancient Egyptians had the sun god Ra and the god of the Nile. As man began to learn to control nature through advancements like aqueducts to channel rivers, the unknown moved more to the heart. What was man's purpose and motivation? So the Greeks created hero gods like

Apollo and Zeus who, while they still controlled nature, were more interested in the moral advancement of mankind. They taught us how we should live and think. Modern man has moved beyond all of that hocus pocus, and our gods have become, in fact, ourselves. There are few unexplained things, and those that are hidden we will soon rationalize thorough scientific study.

> *They exchanged the truth of God for a lie, and worshipped and served what has been created instead of the Creator, who is praised forever. Amen.*
> Romans 1:25

The God we serve is different. He is not defined by what He does, rather who He is. When Moses asked God at the burning bush, "What do I tell the captive Israelites you do? How do I make you understandable to them?" God's response was, "I Am." God is simple. Not simple as in easy to understand or plain. We often assume that if something is simple, it is somehow lacking. In chemistry when something is simple it means that it is composed of only one substance or element; it is not mixed. Everything that God is or does is the fullness of who He is. He cannot be divided into distinct parts where we get to pick and choose how we want to understand or know Him.

Most other gods are ruler gods. The ones that made sure things did what they were supposed to. Our God is distinct; He defined what things were supposed to do. Then He set out to hold those things together until He chooses to end them. It is interesting that of all the things God is, and that we often associate with Him – love, kindness, justice, holiness – the first thing He has chosen to reveal about Himself is that He is a creator. In many ways, it makes sense, because it is the beginning of the story and there has to be someone to tell a story to, but it is more significant than that.

When we read the account of creation in the book of Genesis, we understand it in the context of the timeline of the rest of history. God created this or that, said that it was good, and moved on to the next thing. There is a philosophical idea called Deism that proposes that God set the world in motion and is now sitting back like a clockmaker who has wound the clock of time and is just waiting for the momentum to give out. The problem is that we see and understand time linearly. God is not confined by the limitations of time.

The scripture paints a very different picture. The book of Isaiah says *"I am the LORD, and there is no other. I form* (not formed) *light and create* (not created) *darkness, I make success and create disaster;*

I am the LORD, who does all these things." (Isaiah
45:6-7) That does not sound like a disconnected
God. And He is not done. He is not done creating.

> *For I will create a new heaven and a new
> earth; the past events will not be remem-
> bered or come to mind. Then be glad and
> rejoice forever in what I am creating; for
> I will create Jerusalem to be a joy and its
> people to be a delight.*
> Isaiah 65:17-18

CREATED IN HIS IMAGE

All mankind has been created in the image of God.

Then God said, "Let Us make man in Our image, according to Our likeness."
Genesis 1:26

When God looked at His creation after the fifth day, even though what He had made was good, there was still something missing. The nature of God is founded on relationship. It is seen in the makeup of the Trinity. God the Father, God the Son, and God the Spirit operating distinctly together towards one purpose. Everything created before man served a purpose, but lacked the necessary root of relationship — love. Love requires imagination. Imagination is the source of creativity.

We have all been created in the image of God, and because of that, every person has the ability to create. The ability to create doesn't mean that there is something latent on the inside of us that if we dig real hard and practice for ten years, we can access some "talent" that has been somehow missing in our lives. The ability to create is more like the ability to breathe. It is something that comes naturally with normal brain activity. We create every time we speak a word; we create every time we see something, we create every time we move. Creation begins in our minds, and our brains are a fascinating microcosm of God's creative process. The core component of the brain is the neuron and neurons pass information between each other through an electrical impulse called a synapse. The average human brain has between 100 to 1000 trillion synapses that connect and reconnect, transforming themselves with every new experience.

Every connection we make is an opportunity to create. The greatest minds in human history were not unique because they were different from the rest of us, or made more "in God's image." They learned to connect and reconnect the things they experienced until new patterns and ideas took shape, and then they transformed those ideas into a reality.

Creation is bringing something into existence that was not here before, and while we are never going to create something totally unique, never before conceived (well maybe we can) we are always creating new expressions of what we have seen, even if that creation is only realized in our imaginations. This is where creation starts. When God created the world, He did not accomplish it through trial and error. He imagined in Himself what would be good. Then He spoke it into existence.

Imagination in and of itself cannot accomplish much in the natural realm, so we have to discover how to translate what is in our imaginations into reality. We cannot "see" God. We cannot fully comprehend and understand all that He is. He is, after all, God. But through faith, the supernatural can become natural.

By faith we understand that the universe was created by the word of God so that what is seen was made from things that are not visible.
Hebrews 11:3

Faith and creativity are made of the same substance. It takes the same kind of faith to bring a painting from our minds into reality as it takes for a blind man to see. We just practice one more than the other and have a misplaced understanding of the source of creativity.

THE ART OF RELATIONSHIP

God created us to be like Him. The biblical account of man's creation is magnificent in its picture of God's heart for us. He looked at His creation and saw that something was missing, so He created man. God bent down to the earth He had made and began sculpting and forming the dirt. At this point, besides the new shape of His creation, there was nothing that differentiated it from the rest of the world. It was water and dust. But then God bent down again, and this time instead of speaking the life into being, He "breathed the breath of life" into the shape and man became a living being. God transferred a part of who He was into the life of man.

His desire was that the relationship being built between Himself and Adam would be one of working together to accomplish God's ultimate dream.

This is evident in the work that God gave Adam to do in the garden. God had created all of these unique creatures and given them the instincts to do what they needed to do, but He put it in Adam's lap to name the animals, to use his creative abilities to bring definition and understanding to what God had made.

> *The Lord God formed out of the ground every wild animal and every bird of the sky, and brought each to the man to see what he would call it. And whatever the man called a living creature, that was its name.*
> Genesis 2:19

God formed the creation. Man named it. Creativity comes from the same fabric as prophecy. It is translating God's ideas into man's understanding. (2 Peter 1:21). It is interesting that God has chosen to use us to show Himself and reveal His word to the world. Understand, God does not need us to accomplish what He wills. He is not somehow incomplete without us. But in His wisdom, He has chosen to reveal Himself through relationship.

There are few times in scripture that God physically creates something to reveal Himself. The original 10 Commandments were carved in stone by the hand of God. In the book of Daniel, a hand is sent from the presence of God to inscribe a message to King Belshazzar. The presence of God is often revealed in clouds, fire, and thunder throughout the Old Testament. In most cases, God chose to use the creative faith of His people to reveal Himself. The instructions for the building and operation of the tabernacle is very detailed and takes up many of the pages of the Pentateuch, but none of it was physically built by God Himself. It took craftsmen and administrators to bring God's plan to reality. We will dive into this a little more in later chapters.

Let's take a minute and look at some of God's instructions for the building of the Ark of the Covenant. In Exodus, God commands Moses to build an ark with specific dimensions out of acacia wood. God tells him to cover it in gold and make poles to carry it. Then things get interesting. *"Make a mercy seat of pure gold...make two cherubim of gold; make them of hammered work at the two ends of the mercy seat."* (Exodus 25:17-18) What does a mercy seat look like? Should the cherub be a realistic representation or something figurative? Should they have hard, angled edges, or a soft, rounded profile? We don't know. And God did not specify. What we do know is that there were craftsmen who were filled with the Spirit of

God who set out to make this piece of art. It would seem that the relationship between the Spirit of God and the artist was complete enough to create what God had envisioned. Complete enough that at the end of the instructions God proclaims —

> *"I will meet with you there above the mercy seat, between the two cherubim that are over the ark of the testimony; I will speak with you from there about all that I command you regarding the Israelites."*
> Exodus 25:22

God wants to relate to us through art. We no longer need the confines of a specific building in which to meet with God. Our relationship with Him has moved to something deeper and more personal than that. It would be easy to dismiss the idea that art is still a necessity for relationship. It is, in fact, foundational.

If we understand creativity as translating God's ideas into man's understanding, then the purest form of that creativity is found in the Bible. It may be out of vogue to believe these days, but the truth is the Bible is the inspired, perfect Word of God. And it is art. Unlike the stone tablets, God did not reach down to earth and inscribe the words of the

Bible on pieces of paper. The Holy Spirit breathed on craftsmen who penned epic works of poetry and prose, law and history, letters and decrees. Craftsmen and artists who walked in such a relationship to God that we now understand their art as perfect — as the words of God Himself.

GOD ALWAYS WANTS TO REVEAL HIMSELF THROUGH RELATIONSHIP.

WE CAN CHOOSE TO CREATE WITHIN THAT RELATIONSHIP AND BE DRAWN CLOSER TO HIM, OR WE CAN CHOOSE TO CREATE OUTSIDE OF THAT RELATIONSHIP AND BUILD IDOLS TO OURSELVES.

BROKEN RELATIONSHIP

"No! You will not die," the serpent said to the woman. "In fact, God knows that when you eat it your eyes will be opened and you will be like God, knowing good and evil." Then the woman saw that the tree was good for food and delightful to look at and that it was desirable for obtaining wisdom. So she took some of its fruit and ate it; she also gave some to her husband, who was with her, and he ate it. Then the eyes of both of them were opened, and they knew they were naked..."

Genesis 3:4-7

God longs to have a creative dialogue with man. That is how our relationship was intended to be. But something happened. That dialogue was broken. We chose instead to work from our understanding, to acquire a knowledge of good and evil in the vain hope that it would make us even more like God. Man got the false assurance that he could create his reality, apart from the influx of divine inspiration and direction. Man chose sin, and God can have no part in sin, (Romans 5) so there was a rift between our creative nature and our creative influence. Now the creative process has become about what is created rather than who it is created for, and we have created idols.

Since creativity is something that is accessible to everyone, no matter their understanding or relationship with God, our creative acts then become something of obedience, and out of that our art becomes worship. We are offering back to God what He has given us in the first place, instead of using these abilities for our gain. It is the difference between an altar and an idol. Altars and idols are both objects that are made by man's hands, out of virtually the same materials, with the same creative process, but their purposes are completely different.

Idols, especially when they were created by the children of Israel, were built for man's purposes. Over and over again when the Israelites fell away from God and turned to something else it says they *"built themselves an idol."* (Exodus 32:8, Deuteronomy 9:12, Isaiah 44:15).

Worship is a conscious decision. It affects what we do. What we worship influences what we create.

When the people saw that Moses delayed in coming down from the mountain, they gathered around Aaron and said to him, "Come, make us a god who will go before us because this Moses, the man who brought us up from the land of Egypt - we don't know what has happened to him!" Then Aaron replied to them, "Take off the gold rings that are on the ears of your wives, your sons, and your daughters and bring them to me." So all the people took off the gold rings that were on their ears and brought them to Aaron. He took the gold from their hands, fashioned it with an engraving tool, and made it into an image of a calf.

Exodus 32:1-4

We must take responsibility for what we create. It is not dictated by the muse; it is not dictated by the culture — it is dictated by our hearts. We can often fall into the trap that Aaron did and try to escape the consequences of our actions.

*(To Moses) "Don't be enraged, my lord,"
Aaron replied. "You yourself know that the
people are intent on evil. They said to me,
'Make us a god who will go before us...' So I
said to them, 'Whoever has gold, take it off,'
and they gave it to me. When I threw it into
the fire, out came this calf!"*

Exodus 32:22-24

As incredible as it sounds, this is how we sometimes explain our art. "It was outside of my control. I just followed the brush (or the keys, or the moment)." Idols are created when we lose sight of the source of creativity.

Altars, on the other hand, like in Abraham's case, were built unto the Lord.

*But the Lord appeared to Abram and said,
"I will give this land to your offspring." So
he built an altar there to the Lord who had
appeared to him.*

Genesis 12:7

Abraham made the decision because of an encounter with God to worship Him. It didn't just happen. It was not an accident. It was not without purpose.

THERE IS LITTLE DIFFERENCE IN HOW ALTARS AND IDOLS ARE MADE.

THERE IS LITTLE DIFFERENCE IN WHERE THEY ARE MADE.

WHAT MAKES THE DIFFERENCE BETWEEN LIFE AND DEATH, RELATIONSHIP AND WRATH, IS WHY THEY ARE MADE.

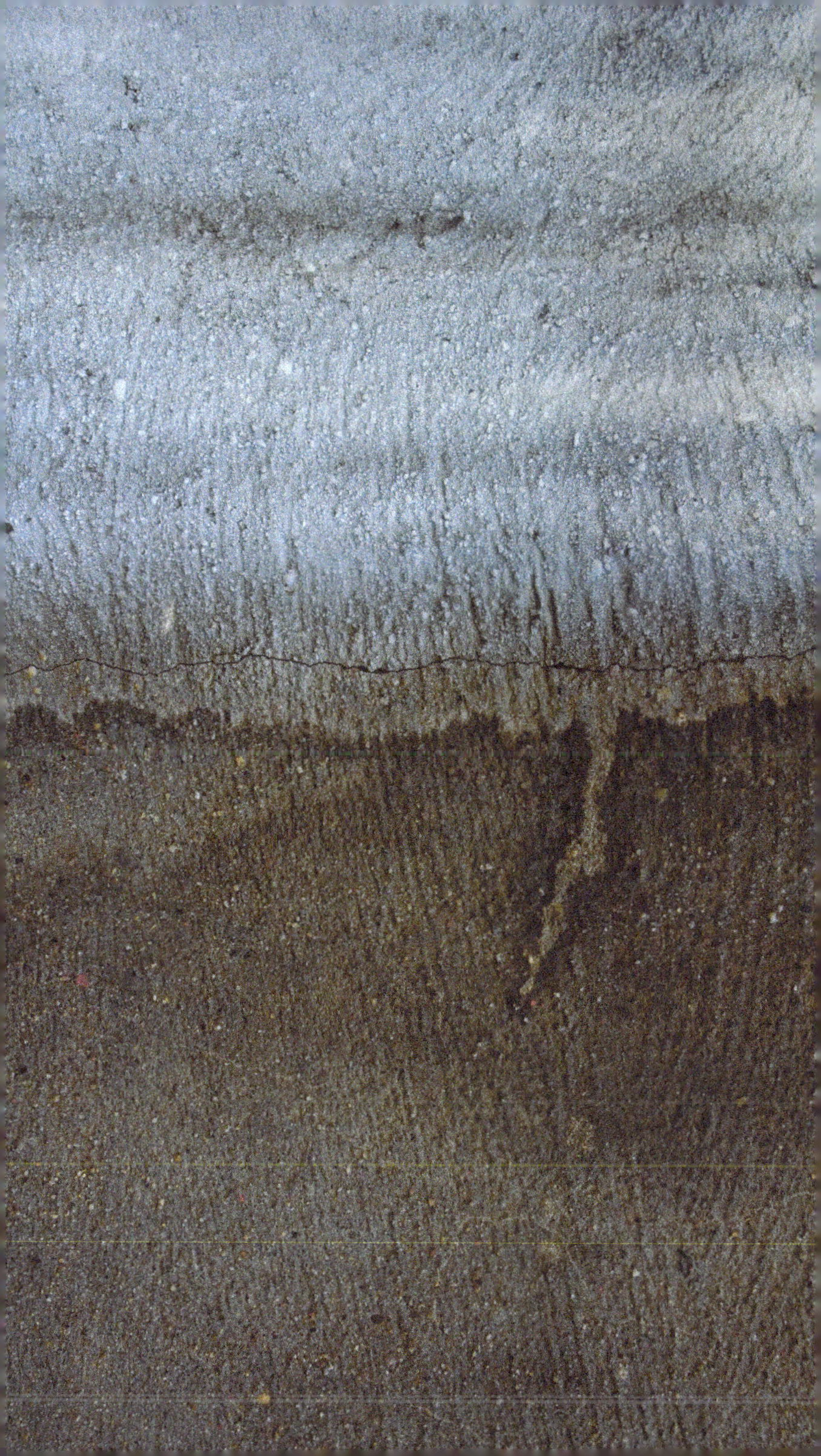

GOD OF RESTORATION

We have to understand that God is a God of restoration. He will not leave us in the place where we are at, especially when that state is opposed to the way that He intended it to be. When God created, it was His word that did the creating. He spoke, and things came into being. Not just land and air and sky and life, but promises and purpose and the future. God can never go back on His word. He will never give up on what He created and called good. It does not matter how many times we turn away and run, or how many apples we eat from the tree, God's purposes will come to pass.

God's mercy does not mean that we can do whatever we want and in the end, it will all turn out alright. Read through the book of Judges. The entire book chronicles the ups and down of the people of Israel. Each new section starts out something like this — *"The Israelites did what was evil in the Lord's sight; they forgot the Lord their God and worshiped the Baals and Asherahs."* Judges 3:7. God's purposes for His people would still prevail, but there were generations of people who did not get to take part in the blessing of relationship. What it is saying is that God knew what would happen. He knew that Adam would make the decision to turn his back on the source of creativity and that a chasm would be formed between God and His creation. So He began a process of restoration, even from the beginning.

All throughout the Old Testament God is working out a path to salvation. He is building a bridge back to Himself. We see it in shadows and prophecies. We see it in tabernacles and temples. We see it in hymns and psalms. Throughout the art of the Old Testament man is trying to get back to that place of creative relationship. But there was still a veil that separated us from face to face inspiration.

Then came Jesus.

The Word. The creative force of the Godhead brought salvation to the creation. It wasn't a re-creation, it was a restoration. Re-creation implies that something was destroyed and something new was put in its place. Yes, death was destroyed, but death was never supposed to be there. Restoration is a return to the original. The word never ended. It will not come back void. In one divine moment, in one selfless act, the veil was rent. The chasm was closed. Jesus, the master creator, brought inspiration back to His creation. His blood was shed, and in a way deeper than the colors we know, red washed us white.

Man was created in the image of God to create. It is our decision to choose what we are going to do with that. If we want to see creativity that is beyond anything we have ever imagined, it is possible. But we have to choose to be washed. We have to look outside of the earthly realm of creative understanding and peer into the supernatural.

SEARCHING FOR SOMETHING

While Jesus has given us a door to access the Father and redeem our creative lives, all humanity has not been made perfect. Without the acceptance of Jesus into our lives and the washing of His blood, we still find ourselves stuck in that place of separation from God. We still create out of our sinful nature. A great poet once wrote —

The eye is not satisfied with seeing or the ear filled with hearing. What has been is what will be, and what has been done is what will be done; there is nothing new under the sun.
Ecclesiastes 1:8-9

Our spirits yearn to be filled. We look continually for something to satisfy the creative space inside of us. In a sense, this statement by King Solomon puts into perspective the state of art and creativity in this day and age. We are constantly searching for something to fill our senses, and because of the way our brains are programmed, we soon forget what we just saw or heard and need a new stimulus to take its place. In some cases, this is a good thing. Imagine if you were able to discern every sound that your ear can hear, continually bombarding you with information. We would have nowhere to focus our attention. We would go insane. Our brains choose those sounds it thinks are the most important and shuts off what is "white noise." The problem arises when the pursuit of new overtakes the pursuit of truth.

In many ways, our creative focus works the same way. We are continually seeking the next big thing or movement that is going to shake the world. We tire of what we have seen. Visual and aural stimulation become something common, and our minds search for a new rush or creative high. We forget that our fresh idea is simply a reworking of something old, something common. Take for example the things that we think of as creative.

Writing – When you break it down, all of our writing in English, (and in many other non-eastern languages) just rearranges 26 letters. The works of great authors, poets, and orators, whose creations can fill vast volumes of books come from only 26 little shapes.

Art – Look at the wonderful masterpieces of Renaissance art. The depth of detail in a Pixar movie. The colors that we see which bring such variety and vitality to our lives are only mixtures of three simple colors.

Music – Music is a language that can transcend culture, transform our lives and capture the spirit of a generation. But when you think about it and figure out how to get past all the majors and minors and diminished and suspended, you find twelve notes.

When King Solomon says there is nothing new under the sun, it is a recognition that our creativity has to start somewhere. Without a relationship to the Creator, we are destined to continually return to the boundaries of "new."

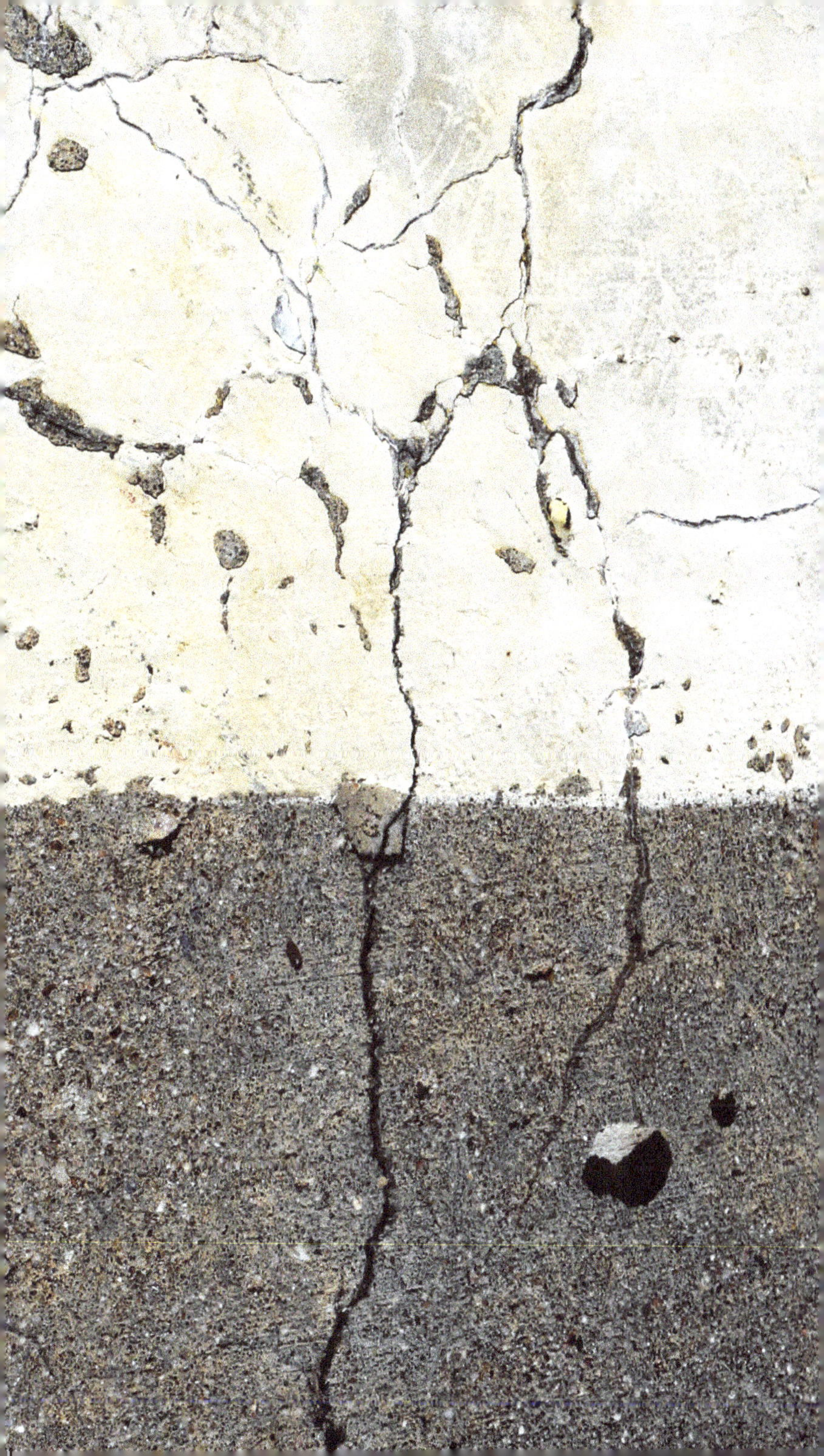

ART WITH A CAPITAL "A"

The understanding that creativity is finite is an important idea to keep in mind when thinking about the way the world looks at and approaches art. Especially Art with a capital A. Art with a capital A is the view that art somehow transcends normal social, philosophical or theological boundaries. It is the idea that art is beyond truth and the Artist the sole custodian of this liberated understanding. The artist has become the new gnostic.

Art and creativity are not ideas that are so vast that they are beyond the understanding of "normal" people. We just need to view them through a different lens. Viewing creativity through a new understanding is not to try and diminish the impact that art can have on people and the importance that it plays in our lives. Art does have the ability to reach different parts of our understanding than the logical, fact based foundations of our western thinking and so it seems magical. But creativity is for everyone. Especially those who walk in relationship with Jesus.

There is no need for this book to take a lot of time trying to confront or explain art as it is understood on a broad scale. The goal is not to change the cultural definitions of what art is and force people into a new paradigm without the foundations of a biblical worldview. Changing everyone's idea of art is not going to bring them into an understanding of Jesus. But when we do have a relationship with Jesus, our understanding of art needs to change. The remainder of this book is an approach for the church to look at creativity from a God-centered perspective, and perhaps redefine some of the thought processes that have made their way into the church and into our minds about creativity, art, imagination and even how we understand God.

Unfortunately, a vast majority of the examples we have to look at concerning how creativity works come out of a worldly understanding and experience. There are excellent resources available that run the gamut on creative thinking and strategies and many are well worth the time to read and study. The problem is that too many times the church simply re-packages a concept and tries to incorporate it into our ministry. Or, as happens far too often, we don't even repackage it and bring corrupt, man centered artistic practices into the church under the guise of "it will help us connect better with the culture."

The problem is that we live in a depraved culture that has bought into the idea that art is somehow exempt from all moral or ethical standards. Art is simply a reflection of the way things are. I don't have control over what I create because I am just translating the "truth" of what is already happening. Take for example a situation that took place at Yale University. A female art graduate student prepared as her final project a performance art piece in which she artificially inseminated herself then used herbal drugs to induce an abortion and used the blood from these abortions as the medium for which to paint her images. Now, there is speculation that the whole thing was faked, and it was simply a publicity stunt, but it was viewed as a legitimate art project. Many people stood on the grounds that it was permissible and even good based on this warped idea of untouchable artistic freedom. And as terrible as this sounds, some viewed it as tame.

Retelling this story is not saying that the church

has gone so far as to fully embrace this type of art or creative expression, but in many ways, the underlying principles of a relative truth and humanistic achievement have seeped in through the cracks. Much of that is due to a lack of understanding about true creativity and its place in God's kingdom. We are simply aware that there is something in us that desires creative expression, so we get it from wherever it is available.

"CHURCH" ART

A discussion on creativity coming from within the church has been problematic to have for some time because, until fairly recently, in many cases it has been completely lost or relegated to a corner. Although it may not have always been communicated this matter of factly, there has been a mindset that because the creative process is so dependent on personal interpretation and human actions it is too easily corrupted. And, unfortunately, in many cases that is the truth. Because there has not been enough understanding or artistic practice within the church, people with creative inklings often feel like they are in free fall. People need structure. Artists need a purpose. Even a free thinking, open to anything artist needs some direction, boundaries, or philosophical framework, and many who started out in the church eventually had to go outside of the church to find a place.

Then there is the "art" that apparently is more palatable to the church. As long as the paintings are of nice lighthouses with pretty sunsets or the dances are choreographed to include the least amount of body movement possible so as not to suggest anything that should not be suggested, we could use those to decorate our bathrooms or do a special song once a quarter. In order to let the creative types have an outlet. Understand, these examples are generalizations and by no means reflect the attitudes of many creative pastors and churches around the world, but unfortunately far too many people live under the impression that this is as far as the church is going to go. The thinking goes something like this: singing in the church choir is great, but if you want to make a difference you need to get a record contract and find someplace where you are actually going to be heard.

In exploring "church" art and its impact on the wider culture, there is one area that seems to be an exception, and that is the area of music. As a source of creative outlet, worship music has found a place of acceptance and nurturing that has enabled it to grow and create an impact even outside the walls of the church. It has become such a part of our church lifestyle that when we hear the word worship what first comes to most minds is melodious sonnets cast up to heaven with outstretched hands. At worship conferences there are tracks on leading worship, writing songs, playing instruments, running sound, etc., etc. All of this is wonderful, but is this where the creative exploration or the ability to touch God end? If we place our focus on one thing for so long and make that action the only means by which to reach God, we can find ourselves in trouble.

Does the Lord take pleasure in burnt offerings and sacrifices as much as in obeying the Lord? Look: to obey is better than sacrifice, to pay attention is better than the fat of rams. For rebellion is like the sin of divination, and defiance is like wickedness and idolatry.
1 Samuel 15:22-23

This trouble was the place where King Saul found himself. God had told him to destroy everything of the Amalekites, but Saul thought it would be a good idea to save some things as a sacrifice. Worship had become the "act" of worship. He forgot that worship is a means of relationship with God. Relationship necessitates communication. Anything — be it singing, dancing, the written word, playing music, painting pictures — that becomes a proxy for communication erodes relationship, and ultimately idolatry replaces worship.

TRI-FOLD WORSHIP

Worship is the outward expression of our relationship with God. It is woven intricately through all of scripture, and it is the bloodline of the body of Christ. A lack of worship is a sure sign of a lack of understanding who God is. When we see Him, we are driven to worship. Isaiah and John both recount experiences of seeing the presence of God and having no other reaction than to fall face down in worship.

Creativity is a means of expressing worship. It is an offering. A recognition that God has granted us something. We are to *present our bodies (who we are) as a living sacrifice, holy and pleasing to God; this is your spiritual worship.* (Romans 12:1) How we understand worship dictates our understanding of how our art attains the place of being holy and pleasing to God.

Worship requires three things – purpose, practice and a place. The purpose comes through prayer and relationship with God. It comes through falling in love with His Word; if we do not start here, or at least end up here, our worship is pointless. People can sing songs of worship without first understanding the purpose, but if their singing does not drive them to a desire for a deeper relationship what is the point of the song?

> *Better a day in Your courts than a thousand anywhere else. I would rather be at the door of the house of my God than to live in the tents of the wicked.*
>
> Psalm 84:10

David did not write this psalm because the words sounded poetic and it would make a good hook for a praise chorus. He wrote these words because he had spent time in the courts of the Lord and longed to remain in relationship with Him.

As we experience more and more of this relationship with God, as we see prayers answered, it drives us to a response. That is the practice of worship. The practice is what we most often associate with the word "worship." Songs of adoration, dances of joy. It takes our inward experiences and brings them outward. How worship is practiced is varied, colorful and vibrant. In scripture we see physical acts of worship; lifting hands, singing songs, shouts of joy, falling prostrate in His presence. We also see sacrifice, caring for widows and orphans, and tithing. Worship can be expressed through songs, dance, literature, theater, oration, and a myriad of other actions. The practice of worship is what brings the community to our relationship with God.

Then there is the place of worship, the atmosphere that focuses our minds and hearts. Place is the aspect of worship that is most often forgotten or misunderstood. Colors and shapes, space and light, the creative space, either physical or spiritual, that allows for interaction with God. This is the place where the artist, like the worship leader, helps to usher the congregation into moments of encounter. The space of worship speaks to the part of our spirit where words lose meaning. God gave us two eyes, as well as two ears so what we see is just as important as what we hear. The place of worship does not have to be physical. We are no longer required to meet with God in a specific space. The necessary thing is the focus.

Where problems come and where we can slip into complacency is when we put imbalanced importance on either the practice of our worship or the place of our worship. Both are needed, and both can be experienced in greater measure in our churches, but when the purpose of worship is minimized or overshadowed by what and how we do it, it is very easy to fall into the same trap as King Saul and everything can be stripped away.

REDEFINING ART

What constitutes art and creativity? As the church, we need to have an understanding of what art is. Not because the current definition is wrong, but because there is a kingdom definition that is better. God has laid out enough things in the Bible that we do not need to simply repackage the cultural understanding to align with what we believe in the Kingdom. There is a need to completely reexamine the subject from the beginning and form our artistic practices out of a biblically based mindset.

When we say art, we are not only talking about painting and drawing. Art in this context also includes music, dance, drama, writing, photography, film, sculpture, architecture, graphic design, poetry — anything that comes through a process of bringing things into existence that were not there before. If we add creativity into the definition, you could even go so far as to include business, evangelism, church planting, pastoring, prayer and things of that nature. One of the problems we have is that our thinking is too small and compartmentalized into left brain/right brain, creative endeavors versus a logical process.

The Church has had a difficult time incorporating creativity in our theology. One reason for this is that creativity is difficult to define and teach. Within the context of our churches, things that reside in our imaginations don't work well for a four point sermon and an altar call. We need to see the eyes of our creative spirit opened and discover how to manifest a picture of God in the earth that is not watered down or one dimensional, but alive and dynamic and growing. At the same time, there has to be a biblical foundation for our understanding, otherwise it is far too easy to be swept around by the currents of new ideas. Paul writes to the church in Ephesus, celebrating the Good News coming to the Gentiles who had formerly been excluded from the body of believers. In his exhortation he paints a picture of God that is far from one dimensional.

This is so that God's multifaceted wisdom may now be made known through the church to the rulers and authorities in the heavens.

Ephesians 4:10

There is room within our theological thinking for an understanding of creativity; we might just need to look at a multi-faceted God from a different angle.

So then, how do we define art in the context of the Kingdom of God? The first problem is that people have a hard time defining art, period. There are even some that say if it can be defined it ceases being art, which, heaven forbid, would make it (or more importantly the artist) less important. Many definitions of art, especially in an American context revolve around the artist. If the artist says it is art and someone believes him and buys his creation or gives value to it in some way, art has been made. Again, this type of thinking perpetuates the idea that being creative is reserved for a few and understanding creativity is limited to those with extraordinary insight. But, art and creativity are definable and accessible, which is seen in the fact that God has placed inside of each of us the ability to create and dream and imagine.

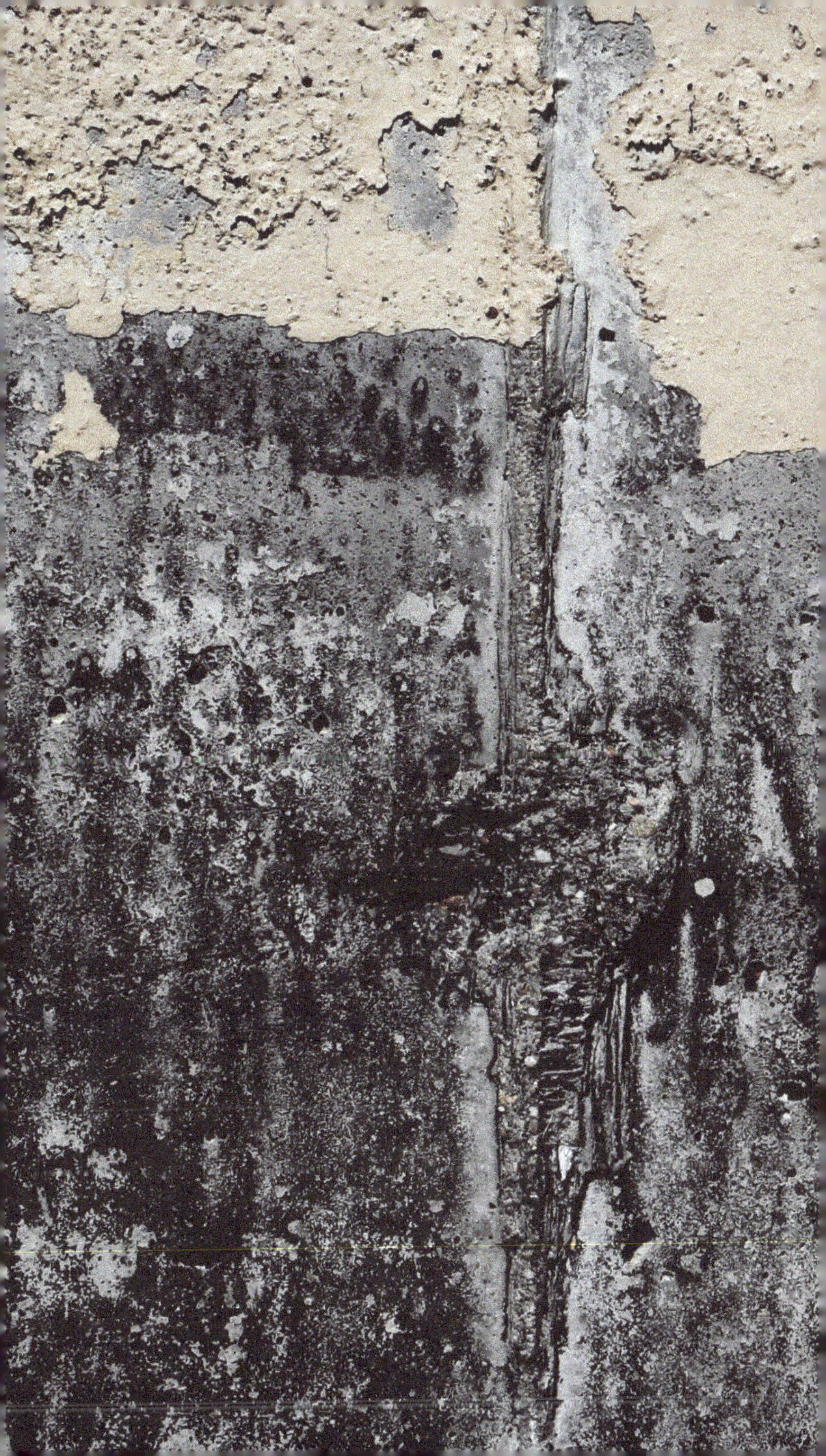

ART IS CREATED

In the next few chapters, we are going to begin developing an understanding of what art is and can be within the context of the Kingdom of God.

Firstly, art is created. This may sound exceedingly obvious, but it is important to understand when we are relating it to how God interacts with us and when our desire is to create to bring Him honor and not ourselves. Art is something that we create, as opposed to nature, which God has created. As great as our brilliant, earth shattering revelation may seem, it is always just a reflection of something that God has already spoken into being. As much as we think of art being an individual endeavor, it is always a collaboration, and God intended it to be that way. Amazingly, God allows us to give the things we create our own expression. Think about it this way: Ten people walk down the street and pass a beautiful tree. It just so happens that all ten of these people are artists and the trees' magnificence drives them to want to create something as an artistic representation of that tree. If you were to gather those people together when they had finished their projects, you would have ten distinct renderings of the same piece of God's nature. Photographs, poems, paintings, melodies, sculptures, dance, scientific explanations, cinematography, sketches or lectures. That is the beauty of divine collaboration.

If the things that we can create must first be revealed to us by God, does that mean that to be creative you have to spend the rest of your life in prayer and fasting, waiting for some audible voice or out of body experience where God shows you things? Doesn't that thinking mean that we are just puppets constrained by a maker who dictates all our actions? Not at all. God has revealed Himself in the things that He created. It is called general revelation. And it is available to everyone. It is not dependent upon our relationship with Him. Even our ability to think and imagine and dream takes place in our minds which are a creation of God.

To say that art is created also has a much less spiritual meaning. Art is not imagination. Art may begin in our imagination, but if that is where it stays, it never becomes art. Creation takes action, and this is the most difficult part. Action is the thing that separates those we view as creators or artists and those we do not. To create art is scary. It requires vulnerability. It requires time and effort. And many times it requires failure. We don't like failure. It has been ingrained in us from an early age that failure is a reflection of weakness. In the church sometimes, failure means you must not have heard God right or listened to what He was telling you. To create art is to break those lies.

Remember that art is a collaboration — at least between God and man. We are created in His image. God is the author of our art, but when we approach the situation through the Blood of Jesus and recognize that we create to bring Him glory, God is also the finisher of our art. God gives us the idea, or we are inspired by His creation, and the Holy Spirit works in the hearts of men to speak the message and change hearts.

**ANYONE CAN
CREATE ART THAT
REFLECTS CULTURE.**

**THROUGH GOD, WE
CAN CREATE ART THAT
DEFINES IT.**

**THE IMPORTANT THING
THOUGH IS THAT WE
CREATE.**

ART IS BEAUTIFUL

The second aspect of art is that it is beautiful. There, it's been said. Art has now been put into a small box that will stifle the creative inklings of musing artists everywhere. "We have to make our art live up to some arbitrary standard." That is not the case. For some reason, people are afraid of beauty. The enemy has so warped our understanding of what beauty is that the church has lost much of its connection with physical beauty. Satan hates beauty. It reminds him of what he lost. When we create beauty, we are bringing restoration to what God set in place.

Beauty is an attribute of God, and as such, He is the fullness of what beauty is and can be. We have watered down our definition of beauty like we have watered down our definition of good. That was a good meal, that was a good basketball shot,

that was a good movie — when in reality the Bible says that only God is good. (Mark 10:18, Luke
18:19) Anything else we describe as that is either
a skewing of the true definition or a reflection
of who God is. It is the same with beauty. True
beauty can only be found in and come from God.
It is out of this foundation that we can make the
blanket statement that our art must be beautiful
because our art must be a reflection of something
that God is. Too often we mistakenly associate
the word beauty with things that are aesthetically
pleasing, but beauty and aesthetics are two different things.

Beauty is based on truth. Truth that is never
changing, not swayed by the current trends or
thought processes of a few. Jesus said that He is
the way, the truth and the life" (John 14:6) and it is
only through Him that we can come to the Father.
That is beauty; the transforming of a dark, lifeless,
separated being, into a living, breathing, son or
daughter of God. Beauty is truth. Aesthetics, on
the other hand, are based on feelings. Take '80's
fashions for example. That is a creative expression
that is totally based on feeling and not so much on
truth. And when the feeling faded we moved on to
another style.

Much of contemporary art culture is based on aesthetics and feeling. This is borne out by the massive number of "movements" that have sprung up over the last 150 years or so. When we look at art history up until the mid-1800's, artistic expression can roughly be divided into time periods. Then came the modern art era and each artist had the freedom to come up with their own style based on aesthetic likes and dislikes. Now we have hundreds of simultaneous "movements" without a common thread. To each his own. But that is the "beauty" of Art, isn't it? Each artist can express themselves completely without being tied to the moor of social whims and culture. Aesthetic differences are not bad. On the contrary, they help make art relevant to particular societies and cultures. The problem comes when aesthetics become the foundation or definition of the "truth."

Beauty is an interesting thing. Most of God's other attributes like love and faithfulness, and goodness, can be experienced by looking through scripture and reading the Bible and feeling the Holy Spirit on us and we begin to understand them in our spirit. God requires creation for His attribute of beauty to be revealed. It is something we interact with through our natural senses. We cannot see love, but we can see beauty, and when we see beauty we get a glimpse of who God is.

We have unhindered access, through Jesus, to the architect and creator of everything, seen and unseen. To say that our art must be beautiful does not put it in a box, but rather gives us the understanding that if we look to God as the source of our creative muse, every person, everywhere, can access something completely new and fresh and earth shattering. And we can do it every single day, for the rest of eternity. That is the basis for our definition of art. Art is beautiful, and beauty can only come from God.

ART BRINGS CHANGE

Finally, art brings change. There are people who say if the purpose of art is to bring change, then it is not art, but simply propaganda. There are also those who say if you try to conform people to a "truth" it is propaganda as well. Jesus says *"the truth will set you free."* (John 8:32) Truth brings change. Beauty is truth. Art is beauty. Art brings change. In creating, we have to understand this principle and use it. The Church is the perfection of beauty in the earth. What is the purpose of the Church? To reveal God in the earth. How do we do that? By representing Jesus in such a way that the Holy Spirit can work in the lives of people and bring change. Art, whether visual, tactile or aural, inherently brings change, even if it is on the most basic level of our conscience. Why would the Church not employ these expressions as a means of carrying the message of Jesus to the world? It's perfect. We do not have to blatantly plaster pictures of Jesus over everything that we create, or write stories based only on scriptures for our art to bring change. The way we create art should be like the way we live our lives. We simply live as God commanded us, loving Him and loving those around us. The form is not the issue. Love is the issue. If our motives are to represent Christ, then the Holy Spirit will do the work in the hearts of people to draw them.

In chemistry, many times for change to take place there has to be a catalyst. A catalyst is a substance that causes or accelerates a reaction without being affected by that reaction. People and situations can also serve as a catalyst. Generally, art does not change. Once something is created it exists until it is destroyed or repurposed for something else. It does not conform to the prevailing mindset of the people who are viewing it. People's interpretation or reaction to art is what changes. This is why the scriptures are such an enduring piece of art. No matter the culture, historical turmoil or misconceptions of the people surrounding it, the Word of God is unchanging.

We need to understand something; as powerful as art is, art cannot save people. Like so many ideas, there is the temptation to take a concept too far and make it into something more than it should be. If that happens, the whole purpose behind the idea is thwarted. While art cannot in and of itself save people, just as someone cannot find true salvation only by experiencing God's creation, art can be a catalyst that brings people to a place of wanting more. This is one of the reasons the local church should be a creator of art. When the Holy Spirit draws people through creativity, there is a place to be drawn to. Then lives can be transformed when the full message of Jesus is presented.

CHANGE IS ONE OF THE REASONS THE LOCAL CHURCH SHOULD BE A CREATOR OF ART.

WHEN THE HOLY SPIRIT DRAWS PEOPLE THROUGH CREATIVITY, THERE IS A PLACE TO BE DRAWN TO.

THEN LIVES CAN BE TRANSFORMED WHEN THE FULL MESSAGE OF JESUS IS PRESENTED.

THE ARTIST CALL

There is one body and one Spirit, just as you were called to one hope at your calling; one Lord, one faith, one baptism, one God and Father of all, who is above all and through all and in all. Now grace was given to each one of us according to the measure of the Messiah's gift.

Ephesians 4:4-7

We have all been given the mandate to use our imagination, and God has placed on the inside of everyone the ability to create, but there are different manifestations for how that creativity is released. Up to this point, we have laid out an overview of the creative attribute that is given to us simply by being created in the image of God. We can all create, and we can all recognize creativity. This section is going to shift focus from the broader creative aspect and explore the calling of an artist.

There are those within the Kingdom of God whose grace is that of the artist. They are the members of the body that are called with the specific purpose of manifesting God through the senses. We are given five senses with which to interact with the world — sight, smell, hearing, touch, and taste. The church has focused mainly on hearing and occasionally on sight. What might we be missing in our experience of God's Kingdom when we don't explore the three and a half senses that are underdeveloped? Take for example our sense of smell. People remember what they smell far beyond what they see or hear. When was the last time you discussed how smells could be used to usher people into the Presence of God? These are things that the artist can awaken. They can speak to the creative longing inside of us and lead others to see new things.

The calling of an artist is not to a specific office. Artists can function as teachers, prophets, evangelists, apostles, and preachers. The artist does not only build into the spiritual house by leading in worship or evangelizing to the unsaved. It may look different than what we are used to seeing, and like many other things in the Kingdom, it may require us to do things that are perhaps outside of our comfort zone. If we can take hold of what God has for us, the possibilities of changing the world are real.

For too long these members have been left to themselves to figure out their place and purpose. In the process they have either shut down entirely or gone on to someplace they could thrive, taking with them valuable pieces of the puzzle that is the Body of Christ. God does not intend for it to be that way. He has given us patterns and directions so that each of us are —

...living stones, being built into a spiritual house to be a holy priesthood, offering spiritual sacrifices acceptable to God through Jesus Christ.

1 Peter 2:5

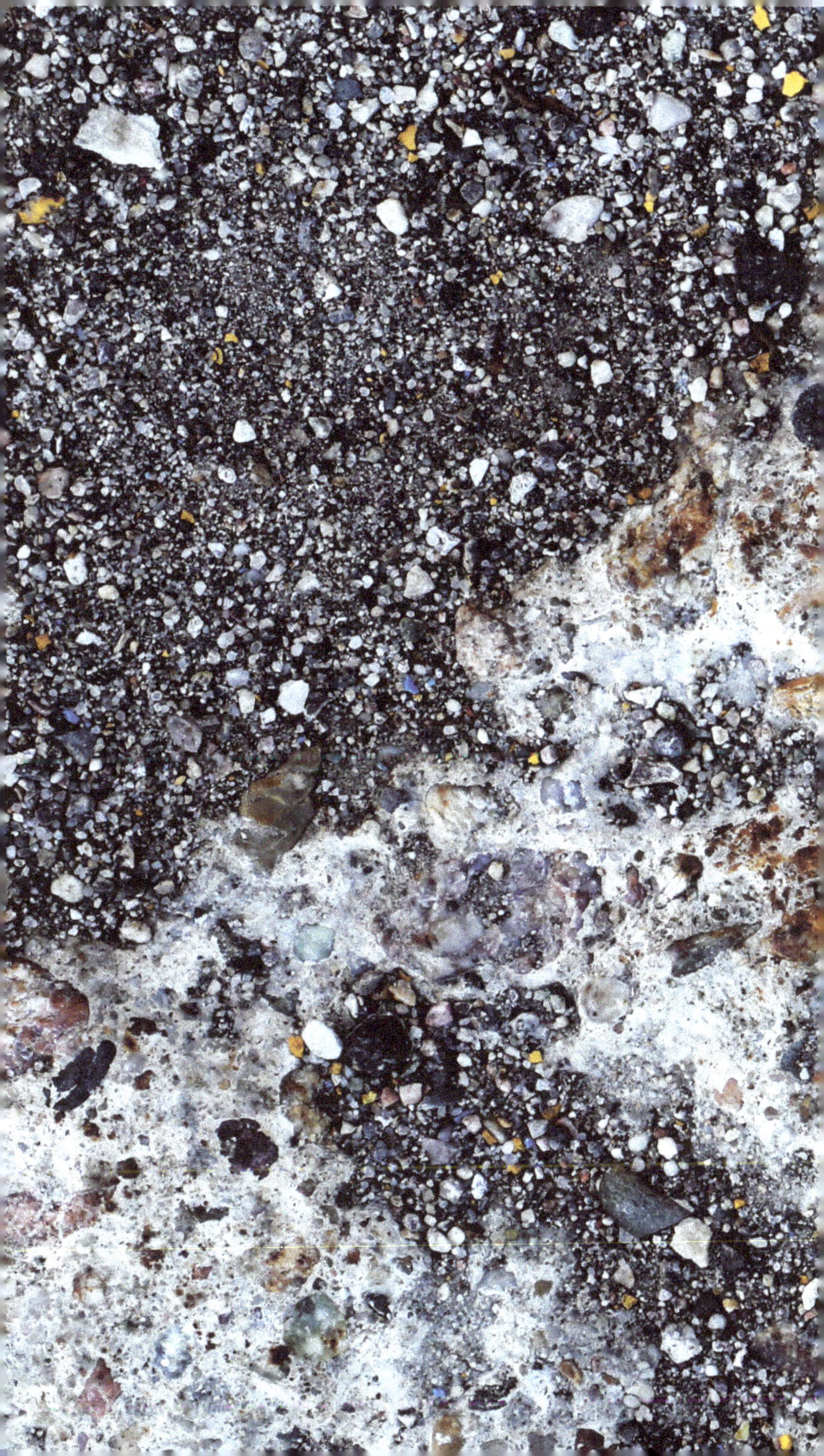

BIBLICAL PATTERN

Moses then said to the Israelites: "Look, the Lord has appointed by name Bezalel son of Uri, son of Hur, of the tribe of Judah. He has filled him with God's Spirit, with wisdom, understanding and ability in every kind of craft to design artistic works in gold, silver and bronze, to cut gemstones for mounting, and to carve wood for work in every kind of artistic craft. He has also given him and Oholiab son of Ahisamach, of the tribe of Dan, the ability to teach others. He has filled them with skill to do all the work of a gem cutter; a designer; an embroiderer in blue, purple and scarlet yarn and fine linen; and a weaver. They can do every kind of craft and design artistic designs."

Exodus 35:29-33

Within this account, God has laid out a pattern concerning how the arts can be implemented within the church. Each church is different, and the makeup of each body is unique in both function and personality, but there are biblical patterns that work universally. Over the next few sections, we will explore some of those patterns and see how to mobilize them within our spheres of influence.

GIFTS AND ABILITIES

One of the first things we see in reading Exodus 35 is that it was the Lord who called Bezalel and Oholiab out from among the people of Israel. It was not something of their own inspiration that drove them to this deep desire to give of their vast abilities to see God glorified through the works of their hands. God called them to this service. We should not take this to mean that the artist is now some sixth fold in church ministry. It would be easy to say, "Look, I have a very important call, now make room for me at the top because what I can do will change the world." The grace of the artist can be manifested in any area of ministry. There is a place within the fabric of the church community for God appointed, highly skilled creators. The problem is that it takes more than an ability to draw a pretty picture. Creators and artists often focus on skill because it is something they can control and it is what sets them apart from the people around them. When we spend so much time and energy on something it can very quickly become the defining part of our lives.

God has given each of us gifts and abilities. His desire is that they are used and fulfilled in our lives, but they cannot become what defines us. You are a creator, or artist, or musician because that is the gift that God has placed in your life, but that is not your life. Like any other work that God has called us to and anointed us for, everything must flow out of a life fully devoted to God and His purposes. *"Out of the abundance of the heart the mouth speaks"* (Luke 6:45), and the mind imagines, and the hands create. When we fill our thoughts and hearts with the simple desire to give to God and follow Him with everything, then when we are creating we will create for Him and not for our own needs.

After God called Bezalel by name, the next thing He did is amazing and is a foundational aspect of the pattern. God filled Bezalel (and most likely Oholiab as well) with the Holy Spirit. The interesting thing about this filling though is that it is one of the first times in the Bible that it specifically mentions someone being filled with the Spirit. And it was not to enable them to speak in tongues. Or to prophesy. Or heal the sick. It was to enable them to create space. To make things beautiful. There was no utilitarian purpose for needing to do this. Yes, they made tables and clothes and utensils, but they were filled with the Spirit for art.

Being gifted is not enough, nor is it the qualifier for work in the Kingdom. If that were the case, we would be able to do the work all on our own. If you spent enough time perfecting your gift, there would automatically be grace for you. We don't know that much about Bezalel before this event happened, but it does not seem like his artistic ability was the primary factor in God's decision to use him. Character, leadership, and a desire for God's people are the necessities for service. And service is what every leader does. Our art is not a great gift to be bestowed on those less fortunate. Our art is meant to help lift others up to a higher place.

We could stop here and have reason enough for artistic expression within the Kingdom, but there are a few other points that can guide us in implementing creativity in the church, while still upholding the foundations that God is after. For creativity to be truly impacting there needs to be structure to it.

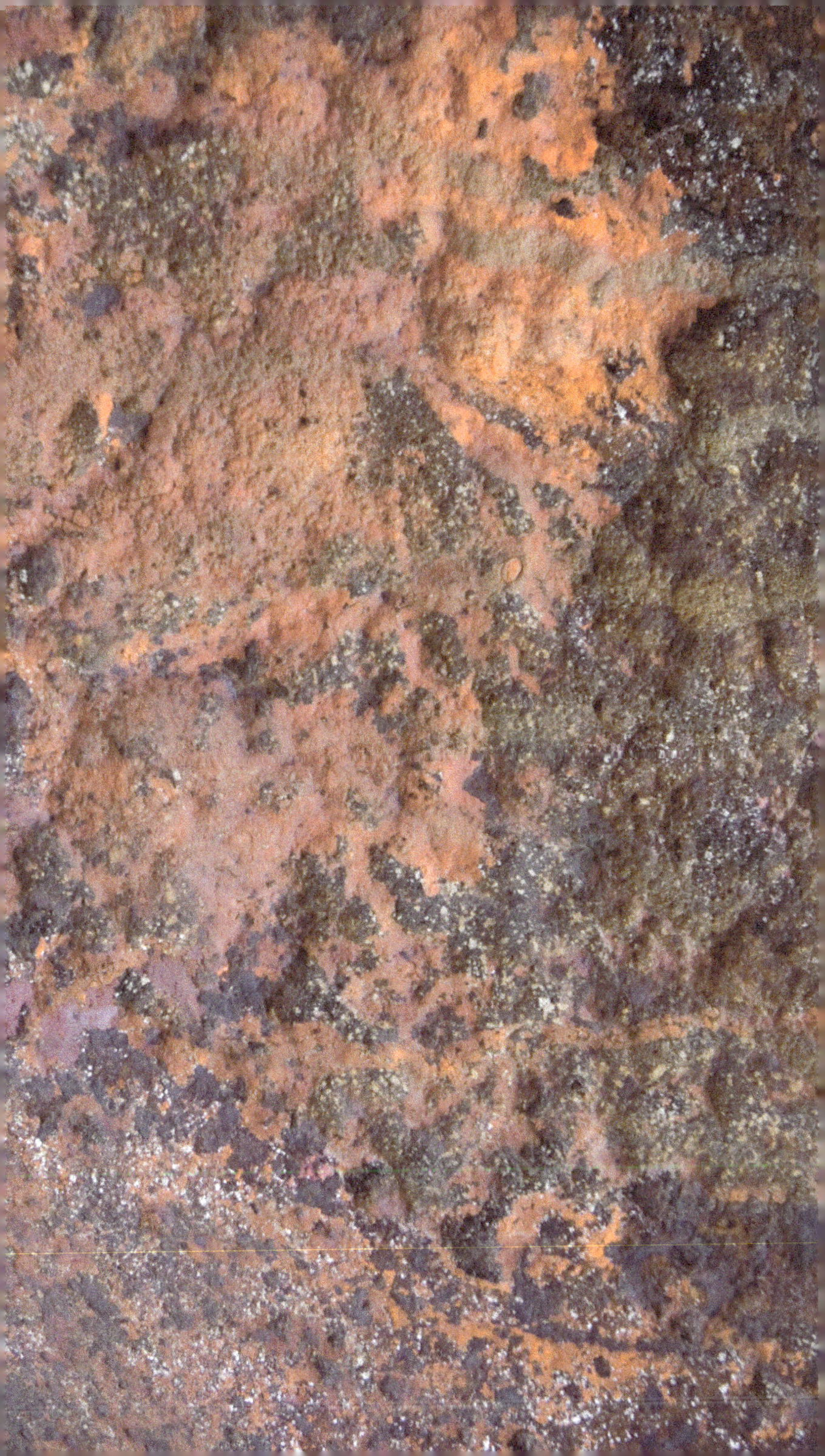

A CREATIVE STRUCTURE

One of the problems with creativity and art in the church is the lack of structure. This is not talking about structure in the sense of aesthetic cohesiveness, but rather the structure of how we practically "do" art. We look at other creative cultures around us and think of them as knowing how to "do" art — probably because they can make money doing it. When the church wants to make a record and get it to lots of people, we use the same patterns as everyone else, simply because we don't know of any other way. But is it the best pattern for the Kingdom? When we need a selection of images to convey an idea or present a message, do we Google through images from any artist willing to offer their work and try to pick the best ones? These may not be bad patterns, but does God have something different, something better in mind.

God not only filled Bezalel and Oholiab with His Spirit, but He also instilled in them a pattern for the creative process. Wisdom, knowledge, and skill.

These three aspects are what is needed for creativity to stay vital, remain grounded, and not lose the power that can be released through creative expression. This is not a random list either, where you can pick and choose what parts you have available, or which pieces are the most important. It is a sequential process. Part of the problem with creativity in the church is that we have the process in the wrong order most of the time. It is pretty much guaranteed that when we think about the arts and especially arts with excellence, the first thing that comes to our minds is a skill. More often than not, this is the aspect that lands people in the positions where they are placed. But this is at the back of the list, the last thing, and something that you cannot have the fullness of without first working through the other two stages.

WISDOM

Wisdom is a communicable attribute of God that He gives to us in pieces. (Psalm 111:10, Proverbs 1:2) Wisdom is the ability to create something with purpose out of what is available, no matter what is available. God created the world in wisdom. He thought of every possible combination of every possible possibility, and the result was the best of all the possibilities. And it was good. Wisdom in creativity is the ability to objectively look at all the creative options and distinguish what is going to have the greatest impact. The thing that is going to bring God the most glory.

For the sake of illustration let's look at the process by which a Hollywood studio creates a film. Wisdom is the producer of the movie. He looks at all the available scripts and chooses the one that he thinks will make the most money. He is the one in charge of making sure that each film represents the values or focus of the studio and finds a director who can carry out that vision.

KNOWLEDGE

Knowledge is distinct from wisdom. The Bible consistently mentions the two together, but as individual functions. (Exodus 35:31, 2 Chronicles 1:10) *"For the Lord gives wisdom, and from His mouth come knowledge and understanding."* (Proverbs 2:6) Wisdom is a heart attribute. Knowledge is perfected in the mind. It is knowing all the steps and processes needed to bring a project to completion. Knowledge is learned and gained from taking part in something, from study. True knowledge needs to come out of a heart of wisdom (Proverbs 15:14) or be filtered through wisdom. Returning to our example of the movie, knowledge would be the director. The director has an understanding of how everything is working together within the context of the project as a whole. He may not be doing every little thing, but there is an understanding of how everything works.

SKILL

Skill or ability is the most outward expression of creativity and as such is often the most praised. Skill is being able to take the subject and materials that have been made available and craft something of significance or value. If wisdom is a heart attribute and knowledge is perfected in the mind, then skill is worked out through the body. It is a training of the muscles to touch the right keys or to put the perfect pressure on a brush. Skill is knowing the right voice inflections to use to make a penetrating point or what order to place the nouns and verbs. Skill is something that is learned and honed over long periods of time. In our movie, the actor or camera operator or key grip would be the example of skill.

COLLABORATION

Collaboration is the key to building a biblical foundation for creativity. To combat the ever encroaching temptations of selfishness and conceit that so easily ensnare the heart of the artist, we have to begin framing the creative journey in a community perspective. Great shifts in society have rarely come from an individual, but one of the great lies the enemy tells us is that we can do it on our own. We were not designed to live on an island, and if our creativity comes only from our inward focus, we will fail to fully realize the life changing power of what we can make.

There is something deeper, something greater that God has in mind. God wants to restore a connection between people as creators. Our relationship with God is the foundation of our creative purpose, but our relationship with each other is the edifice from which that creativity is displayed. The Bible continually equates the church to a wall or a city; something with substance where living stones are built together. We are all familiar with the children's song, "This Little Light of Mine." We are confident in the faith that even if the whole world is dark around us, we are going to continue shining our little lights spread out through this dark and scary world. But that is the second part of the verse, and that light is only able to give light to those in a single house. Jesus starts Matthew 5:14 like this—

> *You are the light of the world. A city situated on a hill cannot be hidden.*
> Matthew 5:14

The effectiveness of an entire city acting as a shelter and guide in a barren wasteland or to ships lost at sea can change entire regions and societies.

To understand the importance of collaboration as it relates to creativity and the creative process, we have to explore how we got to where we are today. We have seen how the selfishness of Adam paved the way for the disconnect that has come between man and the source of creativity. Many people continue to live in that place of spiritual and creative barrenness, even while the connection back to God has been made available through the sacrifice of Jesus. When we let go of our selfish, man centered desires and instead give total control to Christ — not only of our creative capacity but our whole being — life springs forth from that once barren place. There is free access to more inspiration than all of humanity could even remotely come close to thinking up, and every one of us can access it. But this is only half of the story.

What is it that keeps creators so divided? Why has the imagination become something that is hidden deep inside of individuals? The separation between God and man is pretty obvious. We sinned, God hates sin — BIG problem. But while the divide between man and man is rooted in the same issue, the breakup of collaboration has worked itself out a little differently.

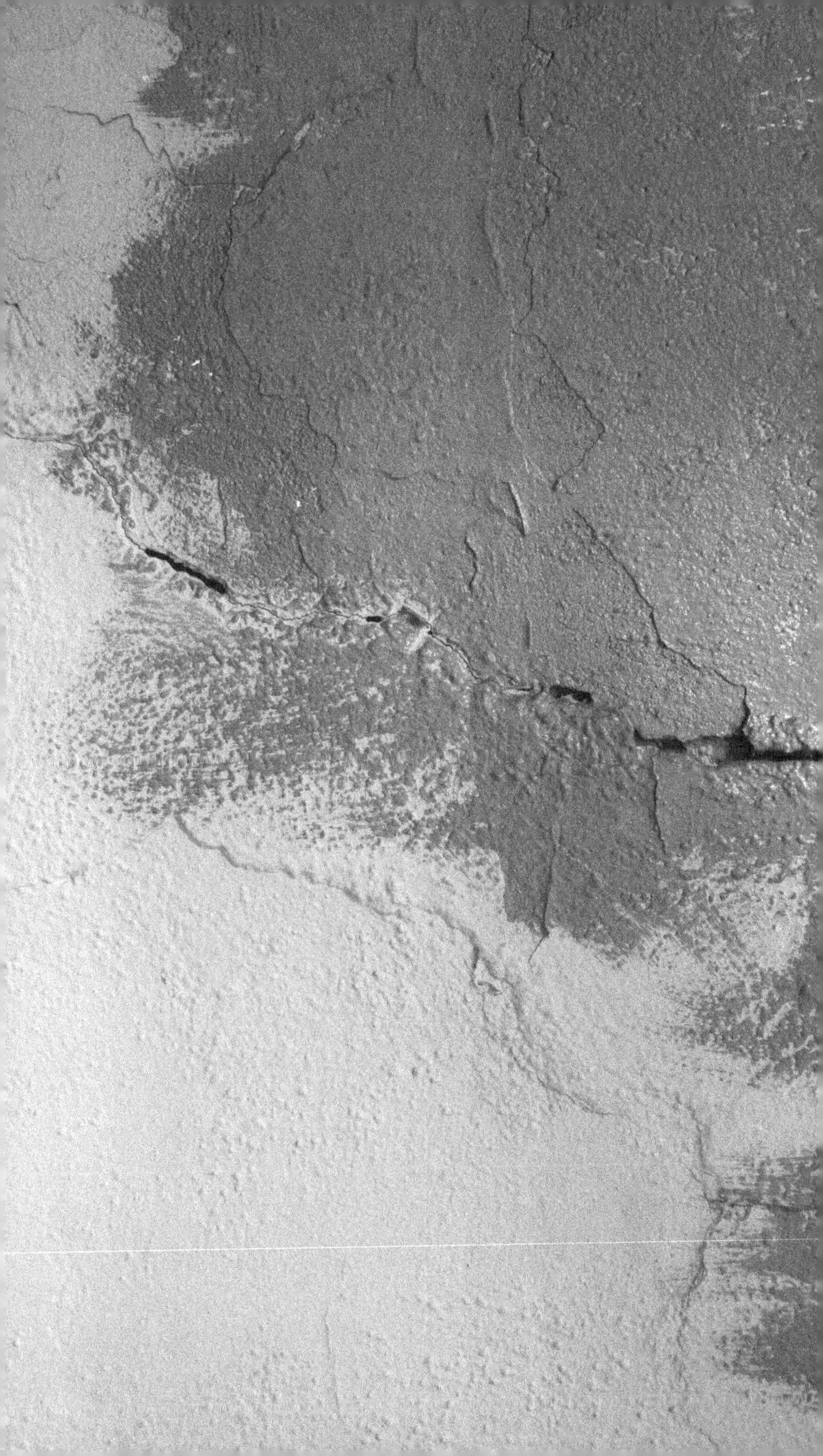

THE TOWER OF BABEL

Following the days of Adam and even after Noah and the flood, everybody on earth had the same language. (Genesis 11:1) That doesn't mean that we all just spoke the same way, we also had the same traditions, same family structures, same geographical location. Our hearts were tied to the same purpose. And that became the root of the problem. We have a God given, innate ability to create and when that desire came together with an innate ability for sin and selfishness given by Adam, creativity itself became a downfall. So man came together and said, "Let us create. We have eaten from the tree and know good and evil, just like God, so let's work together and build a tower, so everyone knows that we are like God. If we create something that is seen and can be understood, unlike this God we serve, nothing can come against us, and we will be served." Thus began the largest creative collaboration in the history of man. An edifice was being built to display man's creativity.

We don't know that much about the Tower of Babel. How big was it really? People have built massive cities and buildings since that time, and God hasn't come down and destroyed them with fire and brimstone. What was it about the building of a city and a tower that made God respond, *"If they are able to accomplish this then nothing will be impossible for them?"* (Genesis 11:5) It had something to do with the power of together. The power of collaboration. What mankind was creating was an alternate to the perfect garden that God had set forth for man to live in; a place where man could rule, but not be under the "authority" or "constraints" placed on them in the garden. They would be able to work together to create out of their abilities and because everyone was able to communicate and interact and understand on the same level, what could be accomplished was so much greater than one man could do on his own.

God saw the potential that He had purposely placed on the inside of His creation, to enable them to draw closer and understand Him, being twisted and fashioned into something that had no hint of godliness or "good" in it. And He had to stop it, not because it was a threat to Him, but because in the end, it could not accomplish God's plan. Stopping it had to have broken His heart just as much as when He had to drive man out of the place of perfect communion with Him. He had designed us to work like Himself — distinct parts, but so closely drawn together in thought and intent that we were like one body. In that design, there could be no place for sin and selfishness, no place for division.

TO ULTIMATELY
REALIZE THE GOAL
THAT WAS SET FORTH
AT THE CREATION OF
MAN, GOD CONFUSED
OUR LANGUAGE.

HE SCATTERED OUR
THOUGHTS.

HE BROKE OUR
COLLABORATION.

RENEWED HOPE

As we have learned from man's experience with separation from God, there is always hope. God's words are never returned to Him void and the desire to bring people into creative wholeness, with Him and with each other, is going to prevail. Through the blood and sacrifice of Jesus, we are now able to have access to God. So what about collaboration? What about a people? Where is the redemption of the creative community? The thing that destroyed the process at the Tower of Babel was not that the people were working together. It was not necessarily that they had one heart and mind. As a matter of fact, God's desire is that we would all have the same heart and mind and language (Acts 4:32), but it is not for our own purposes, it is meant to bring greater glory and honor to God. The tower was built only for the glory of man.

Take a moment to imagine what would have been possible for man to create if, over the centuries, we would not have had the cultural and language barriers that divide people and thought. Think about the massive advances in technology, government, and learning when the Roman Empire began building roads and connecting people that up until that time had no common culture. Look at the quantum leaps that have occurred even in the last 20 or 30 years through technologies that have allowed people from all over the world to begin sharing ideas and working together. These are only shadows of the Kingdom.

Now, take a deep breath and dream about what would be possible through a people that had the same vision, spoke the same cultural language and were all of the same mind — to create to glorify a magnificent God. A living organism where each cell had a direct connection to the life-giving force of creativity, working not for their own glorification, but for something bigger. The collaboration that was broken at the Tower of Babel is being restored through the Church.

A COLLABORATIVE
CHURCH ISN'T JUST
SEVERAL PEOPLE
WORKING ON THE
SAME PROJECT
TOGETHER,
A COLLABORATIVE
CHURCH AND A
COLLABORATIVE
PEOPLE ARE THOSE
THAT WALK TOGETHER
WITH THE SAME
PURPOSE AND THE
SAME HEART.

GOD HAS ESTABLISHED SOMETHING THAT WILL DWARF BABEL.

HE IS BRINGING A KINGDOM THAT WILL STRETCH FROM HEAVEN TO EARTH.

AND WE ARE A PART OF IT.

BIBLICAL COLLABORATION

At its root collaboration is one of the primary focuses of Christianity and the Kingdom, so why would we think that something like creativity or art could somehow exist outside of that pattern? It is through a pattern of collaboration outlined in scriptures that creativity will find its ultimate outlet. We are all one body fitted together in Christ, but each part has a different function. (Romans 12:5, 1 Corinthians 12, Ephesians 3-4) That doesn't mean that each part is separate, it just means that each part is unique in its outlet, but for a unified purpose.

The creative process today has become so far removed from a concept of biblical collaboration that it is difficult to wrap our minds around how creating within this environment is possible. What is needed is a reexamination of some core biblical principles such as wisdom, knowledge, skill, leadership, discipleship, community, and so on to see how they can be practically applied to creating a collaborative culture within a local church. This outline is not a step by step guide. What works well in one church's culture may not be the right fit for another. Methods adapt — principles create the foundation.

First of all, we need to reverse our priorities. For what we create to be the most impactive and possibly life changing, our focus needs to shift from being fixated on the form to strengthening the substance. Why are we creating what we are creating? Is it for personal worship time? That is wonderful and necessary, but is anyone else going to see what you created? Remember, art brings change. What are you communicating in your art? The need to know what we are communicating multiplies when we talk about the church or the collaborative process. Do people see something of substance when they look at the finished product or are they simply seeing a conglomerate of a bunch of artists? Within a local church, is the art enhancing the mission and values of that body?

There needs to be wisdom. There needs to be a purpose. There needs to be a direction. Church leaders need to begin to take hold of and cast vision and direction, not for exactly what needs to be done, but what needs to be said. One of the aspects of wisdom that falls on those with leadership is release. There is often a bottleneck in the creative process between those with the direction and those with the skills. One doesn't know how to release, and one doesn't know how to receive. Those in leadership positions either don't see the necessity for a creative direction, or they don't know how to accomplish it.

Micromanagement does not work in collaboration. Each part needs to be able to fully explore the possibilities within a project for the result to have the depth and life that it needs. On the other hand, many times people with the skill find it difficult to work out of someone else's vision. They look at it as an attack on their own abilities and creative expression. Creative people have gone so long pulling their creativity out of themselves, that they don't know how to work when the inspiration comes from somewhere outside. First, we need to discover how to access God for creative inspiration — and listen to what He says. Then, when the situation warrants it, learn how to take inspiration and direction from others. For collaboration to work, each member of the team has to come to the place of "what I am a part of is more important than the part I play." It may seem overused, but it is true.

The next piece in the creative, collaborative process has been mostly missing altogether. Wisdom and skill have been reversed in their priorities, but knowledge has been thrown out or at least misunderstood. Knowledge in the creative process is the middleman, the organizer, the translator between vision and action. There are pieces of both wisdom and skill. Knowledge is the area that is the most difficult to walk in. There is enough wisdom to come up with your own ideas and enough skill to be able to accomplish them. The person with knowledge ends up trying to do everything and thereby waters down both the message and the vehicle. Many people that are in church staff creative positions find themselves stuck in this place. They know something needs to be done, they know how to do it to a degree, so they do it. Beginning to end. And they get burnt out on it. What is needed is a group of people in the creative process that can translate a vision and set people to work on it, giving specific direction and organization to a group of skilled people. It takes a distinct type of person to successfully walk in and accomplish the things needed to organize a group of creatives, whether it is two people or a team of fifty, but when this piece is in place, the collaboration process can work in a way we don't often experience.

Now, what do we do about all those insanely skilled, insanely independent artsy people? Do we hang them out to dry because they don't have the complete vision? Do we run them off so that they go find an outlet someplace else? Or do we disciple them? One of the most difficult things to ask of a creative person is to create out of someone else's vision. Isn't it interesting that the most difficult thing to ask a person who has lived their entire life in sin and selfishness to live by Jesus' rules? We don't throw out the new believer because it is hard, we disciple them. It takes the same process to bring a person creating completely out of their skill and come into creating as part of a collaborative team. Working in collaboration will also free the skilled artist to be able to concentrate on their craft. If someone who is highly skilled at music is asked to coordinate and direct a group of painters, which he may have no understanding or skill in at all, it could impact his time and effort being put into the music and negatively affect both disciplines. When a skilled person can give everything they have to what they are skilled at, that freedom and focus can create masterful workmanship.

It takes wisdom to
release direction.

It takes knowledge to
guide the way.

It takes skill to
accomplish the task.

Collaboration.

ART FROM THE CHURCH

God wants to bring a restoration of creativity in lives of individuals as well as the local church. It was His plan from the beginning to have people who think and create like Him. The Family of Jesus is the hope of the world. It says in Matthew that we are a light on a hill that shines the light of God for the nations to be drawn to. There is something else that the church is that we don't talk about very often, but in Psalm 50:1 God is speaking, and He says *"God, the Lord God speaks, He summons the earth from east to west, from Zion the perfection of beauty, God appears in radiance."* In the chapter of "Art Brings Change," it mentions in passing that the Church is the perfection of beauty on the earth. This scripture is where that idea originates. Zion, as we will see in a moment, is a picture of what God desires His church to be. The book of Revelation shows us a picture of something that is going to happen, but in other aspects it a picture of what is already happening. There is a saying used in some circles that describes the Kingdom of God as "Already, but not yet." John in his revelation of Christ is showing us a picture of what the church is going to look like, but also what God desires the church to be.

> *I did not see a sanctuary in it because the Lord God the Almighty and the Lamb are its sanctuary. The city does not need the sun or the moon to shine on it because God's glory illuminates it, and the lamp is the Lamb. The nations will walk in its light, and the kings of the earth will bring glory into it. Each day its gates will never close because it will never be night there. They will bring the glory and honor of the nations into it. Nothing profane will ever enter it: no one who is vile or false, but only those written in the Lamb's book of life.*
>
> Revelation 21:22-27

In regards to the arts and creativity, what we see here is that we don't need to bring the things of the world into the church and try to clean them up to make it work for the church. We have tried that over and over. It has brought some change. There is an impact that art and creativity being brought in and transformed can make. It can take people to a place in worship and a place of touching God, but what God wants to do instead is bring an outflow from the church of creativity that goes into the nations. You can see an outline of what this might look like if you continue reading into Revelation chapter 22.

Then he showed me the river of living water, sparkling like crystal, flowing from the throne of God and of the Lamb down the middle of the broad street of the city. On both sides of the river was the tree of life bearing 12 kinds of fruit, producing its fruit every month. The leaves of the tree are for healing the nations, and there will no longer be any curse. The throne of God and of the Lamb will be in the city, and His servant will serve Him.

Revelation 22:1-3

The church being involved in the arts is not something that we need to do just because it is a contemporary, relevant way to reach people. We cannot fall into that. The church should not have projections and lights and music and atmosphere just because it is going to help draw people in and

be relevant to our society. The church should create art because from the church comes the perfection of art. The purpose of art is not just to make
aesthetically beautiful things. The purpose of art
is to reveal the truth. And that is why we create.

CREATIVE COMMUNITY

How do we translate the ideas of wisdom, knowledge, and skill into what we do as a creative community? You can probably think of several people who are too talented for their own good. It becomes what defines them because they find acceptance and praise for it, but their talent has no direction, no purpose and they find themselves wandering through life looking for the next creative high. Are people like this just left to wander, leaving the church in a place of having to find someone with less talent, but a deeper sense of community? On the other end of the spectrum, there are people who can see great and awesome things in their minds and in some cases those plans could probably change the world, but they don't know how to bring those dreams into reality. They are left with their dreams, and the world suffers for it. Are people like this just dreamers?

God has placed us in community and family for a reason. While He may have instilled all three qualities of wisdom, knowledge, and skill into Bezalel and Oholiab, that does not mean that they were the only ones who could do any of the work. In Exodus 36 it begins to list all of the people with skill who were able to help with the building of the tabernacle and its pieces. God has given us relationships so that as a people we can walk out wisdom, knowledge and skill.

Creative people are as much in need of the church as the church is in need of creative people. The creative expression that is able to come forth from community is a multiplication of what we could produce on our own. The thing that is instrumental for this to work is each piece of the puzzle being more committed to the final product than they are concerned about their own part. For this to happen our concern has to be for the heart of the artist. If we forget about discipleship, we can easily find ourselves building tools for a job rather than sons and daughters.

FOSTERING THE HEART

The primary function of a creative church is to foster the heart of the artist. We are here to disciple. We are here to build up. The church is made up of people, and for a church to be creative, the people that make up that church need to be creative. Legally in the United States, an organization or business can be recognized as a person. The individual lives of the people that make up that organization are lumped together and how they think, act, or believe are irrelevant to the ongoing existence of the whole. The church does not work that way. A church can't be something that its people are not.

When we talk about discipling the artist, the focus is not how we help this person draw a better picture or be a better dancer or make better music. Discipleship is about how we help this person find God, and from that place, they are able to work out their art. If you can transform the heart of an artist, you can transform the artist's art.

Discipling the heart of the artist is a unique thing. We want to see people grow in their relationship with God, but many artists experience God through their art. If you are going to start a discipleship group like we are used to doing in the church, you could sit in the corner of the room on a couch to do a Bible study and talk about the scripture and pray with each other. If you are going to disciple a dancer, you need to touch them when and where they dance. And to dance you need to have space for dance.

Let's explore a practical example of how this might look. Dancers are exacting people and the more proficient they become, the more exacting they get. This is not necessarily a deficiency. If the church is to become the perfection of beauty, there is a level of excellence that is necessary to get there. Dancers cannot dance well on carpet. Dancers cannot be thrown through the air in a room with 8-foot ceilings. If we are going to see dancers grow in their relationship with God through their dance, the church needs to disciple in a space where dance can happen.

There are specific needs that are beneficial to address in the process of fostering the heart of the artist. For artists to create, space and equipment are essential. In many cases, it might seem like a waste to have massive rooms for making movies or recording music that sit empty for periods of time, but sometimes that is what it takes.

Many churches do not have the facilities or resources to provide spaces like these, but that does not mean they are unable to disciple artists. Perhaps they just need to start a Bible study in a community studio space. The primary element in discipleship is time and love. Fostering the hearts of artists requires pastors who understand the needs and the pitfalls of the creative life. We need to look at how the enemy comes and uses our creativity against ourselves. As much as God desires us to be a creative people, the enemy knows how to twist things so that what is meant for our growth can turn into our demise. A creative church needs leaders who can recognize and understand the things that come into the hearts of creative people and help to begin to disciple and teach and transform artists so that they can see it in themselves.

DIVERSITY

A creative church is diverse. What this means is, we can't just focus on what we are doing today. The church has a tendency to get stuck behind the movement of culture rather than leading that movement because we get preoccupied with sustaining what we already have. This is a curiosity. It could have something to do with our fear of failure or thinking that change means we have somehow missed God. Either way, our proclivity toward sameness hinders the advancement of the Kingdom. God stays the same in the essence of who He is, but His vastness makes each new moment with Him new for us.

In the book of Exodus, we meet Moses as he encounters God manifesting Himself in a burning bush. God has heard the cries of His people living in captivity in Egypt and has chosen Moses to lead them into freedom. So, Moses goes to Pharaoh and the way we usually retell the story proclaims loudly, "Let my people go." In reality, there was more to the demand.

> *Then the Lord said to Moses, "Go in to Pharaoh and tell to him: This is what Yahweh says: Let My people go, so that they may worship Me."*
> Exodus 8:1

Moses comes to Pharaoh over and over again while Pharaoh continues to harden his heart to God. As plagues rain down on the land of Egypt, Moses comes to Pharaoh again and says, *"Let my people go so they may worship me."* This was the eighth wave of destruction and Pharaoh has had enough — "OK, only the men may go and worship the Lord." Moses tells the king that everyone must go but Pharaoh refuses, and another plague strikes. Moses comes back a ninth time and conveys what the Lord has said, *"Let my people go so they may worship me."* Pharaoh gives in more this time, *"Go worship the Lord, even your families may go, but your flocks and your herds have to stay behind."* The response by Moses is amazing. He says, *"You must also let us have sacrifices and burnt offerings to prepare for Yahweh our God. Even our livestock must go with us; not a hoof will be left behind because we will take some of them to worship Yahweh our God... We will not know what we will use to worship Yahweh until we get there.*" (Exodus 10:25-26)

The Israelites needed all their resources available — all their men, all their women, all their children, all their livestock, all their possessions had to be with them when they went to that place of worship because they didn't know what God was going to require of them. They wanted to be prepared when God says, "This is what I want for worship." When Pharaoh finally relented after the deaths of the firstborn and the Passover, the Israelites left Egypt with all of their possessions. But they also plundered the gold and silver and resources of Egypt. As you read through the Old Testament, the Israelites go into the wilderness and build a tabernacle, a place where God is going to dwell, a place where worship can continually happen. When God said, "This is what it will look like," the Israelites had everything available that was needed.

We have to foster all the creative avenues that are available to us. We don't know when God is going to say "I want this." There are things inside of people's hearts that don't seem to have an outlet right now.

THERE ARE DANCERS CLOSED OFF IN HIDDEN DANCE FLOORS TOUCHING GOD THROUGH MOVEMENTS THAT HAVEN'T YET BEEN CALLED FOR IN CORPORATE WORSHIP.

THERE ARE MUSICIANS IN THEIR ROOMS CREATING SOUNDS FROM HEAVEN THAT HAVE NEVER BEFORE BEEN HEARD ON EARTH.

DO NOT STOP.

ONE DAY GOD WILL SAY, "I WANT THIS."

EXPERIENCING ART

We create art out of a heart of worship, but art is more than just worship. There are times when art needs to be experienced as much as it needs to be created. Art can be prophetic. Art can be proclamatory. Art can teach. Art can do all of these different things. Art is not just worship. Art comes from a heart of worship, but art can be many, many things. Art can be the key that opens the door in people's spirits to allow the Holy Spirit to begin to work. The Holy Spirit is not going to come busting down doors to say something; he needs to be invited in. Sometimes people don't have the words to express the invitation, but what art can do is cause people to ask questions, and a question is an excellent invitation for the Holy Spirit. If we can begin to open doors, God can begin to speak into people's hearts and lives.

GENERATIONS

Creativity is not just for young people, especially when we are talking about the creative process in an atmosphere of collaboration. Part of the problem in creativity and art today, both in the church and especially outside of it, is the lack of substance. A lot of that is due to a lack of wisdom about life. We cannot care so much about being "relevant" that we throw out the lessons of the past because of aesthetic preference. People who have "been there and done that" bring the patina to a creative project that makes it real. If we are to create in the timeless, we cannot only create for now and the future, we must also create from the past. We have to create out of timeless relevance, touching the hearts of this generation with the truths of the past while building for the future.

CONCLUSION

As I end this book, I want to leave you with a few thoughts, the first of which is simply a reiteration of something I started out with. God is really big. He has purposes and plans that are so far beyond our comprehension that to delve into and discover them will take billions of people the rest of eternity and then we will only scratch the surface. To somehow think we can out-create or out-dream that is to place ourselves on much too high a plane. It was attempted at Babel. It was what got Adam into the mess where he found himself. On the other end of the spectrum, our God is one who desires to be known. He longs for His people, His children, to explore the deepest parts of Him. As we draw close to Him, our eyes can be opened to the magnitude of creative possibilities that are contained in the word GOD. Isn't that what worship is? That is what art is. That is what creativity is.

There is a story told by Sir Ken Robinson in the book "Out of Our Minds." In the story, there is a young girl in an art class. When the teacher comes over to her and asks what she is drawing, the girl answers, "I am drawing a picture of God." To which the teacher replies, "But no one knows what God looks like." To which the girl replies,

"They will in a minute."

That is the goal of our creative endeavors. To be salt and light. A city set on a hill. Mount Zion, the perfection of beauty. To do that we have to have the faith of a child. All children dream. All children imagine. A child can be anything they want to be, simply because they don't know they can not. We need to be reborn into our creativity. Take away everything we have "learned" to be the "truth" and simply make-believe.

Finally, where do we go from here? I have many more questions than answers as I come to the end of this book. I don't know exactly what God wants to do, but I do know He desires to do it through His people. My hope in putting these thoughts together was to begin a dialogue, to strike a match. The answers and techniques and tools and people are all out there; they just live in dreams at the moment. Don't be afraid to dream. Don't be afraid to imagine — if we are filling our hearts and minds with the things of God and have been washed white with the blood of Jesus, out of the abundance of our hearts our mouths will speak. Our feet will dance. Our hands will create. God has given us permission because He has given us His Son.

ABOUT THE AUTHOR

CALEB PALMER is the Creative Director and Youth Pastor at Restoration Church in Casper, Wyoming. Previously he worked for many years in the graphic design industry creating web and print visuals for businesses and non-profits. He trained in film production at Maine Media and graduated from Northeast Missouri Bible College (currently Heartland Christian College) with a degree in Biblical Studies. His love for photography and the church has sent him around the world documenting what God is doing. He and his wife Rebecca have three amazing kids — Ethan, Ava and Hudson.

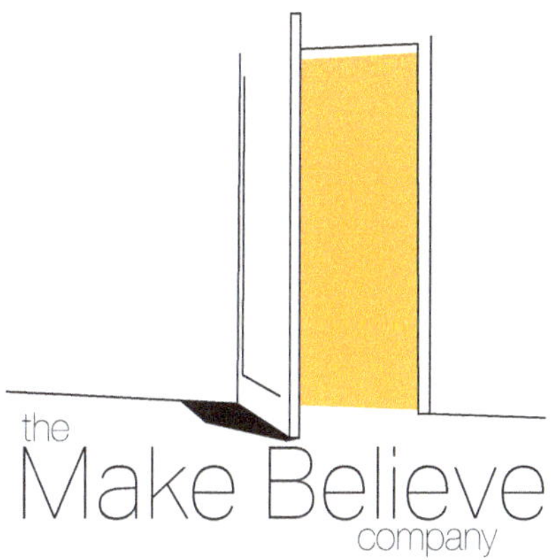

the
Make Believe
company